Haunted New York City

D1310225

0 11557 03471 4

Haunted New York City

Ghosts and Strange Phenomena of the Big Apple

Cheri Revai

Illustrations by Heather Adel Wiggins

STACKPOLE BOOKS

Published in 2008 by
STACKPOLE BOOKS
5067 Ritter Road
Mechanicsburg, PA 17055
www.stackpolebooks.com

Printed in the United States of America

10 9 8 7 6 5 4 3 2 1

FIRST EDITION

Cover design by Caroline Stover
Illustrations by Heather Adel Wiggins

Library of Congress Cataloging-in-Publication Data

Revai, Cheri, 1963–
    Haunted New York City : ghosts and strange phenomena of the Big Apple / Cheri Revai. — 1st ed.
        p. cm.
    Includes bibliographical references (p.).
    ISBN-13: 978-0-8117-3471-4 (pbk.)
    ISBN-10: 0-8117-3471-4 (pbk.)
    1. Haunted places—New York—New York. 2. Ghosts—New York—New York . I. Title.
BF1472.U6R4785   2008
133.109747'1—dc22
                                                        2007025890

To my sisters,
Chris Walker, and C.J. Barry

Contents

Introduction

WHEN ITALIAN GIOVANNI DA VERRAZZANO FIRST HAPPENED UPON THE New York Harbor in 1524, the area was inhabited by Native Americans, including the Manahattoes, for whom Manhattan was ultimately named. But it wasn't until after Dutchman Henry Hudson explored the New World for a merchant group called the Dutch East India Company in 1609 that word of the promising undeveloped region really spread. In 1614, the first Europeans opened a Dutch fur-trading post on the southern tip of what is now Manhattan, and other settlers quickly followed. If you think it's a jungle out there today, you should have seen it in those days, when heated Indian massacres, unicorn sightings (yes, unicorns), and pirates were not so rare, and the primary occupations involved harnessing and using the rugged wilderness through lumbering, farming, and trapping. But that didn't deter Peter Minuet, the Dutch leader appointed to the New World, from purchasing the city from the Canarsees Indians in 1624—for nearly nothing, I might add.

Some sources say the island was traded for $24 worth of glass beads. Though that is believed to be incorrect, it is indisputable that the deal struck by the early Dutch for New York City was the deal of the millennium, considering that at the time the city's population was five hundred, and today it is over eight million and growing—making it one of the ten most populated cities in the world and easily the largest city in the United States.

During Dutch rule, the New York City area was called New Amsterdam, and the modern-day eastern states from Delaware to New York and Connecticut that were being settled by the Dutch were known collectively as the colony of New Netherland. Dutch rule over New Amsterdam and New Netherland lasted only forty years before the English acquired the land in 1664 by forced surrender of the Dutch, renaming their prize New York after James, duke of York.

From the start, the city had been recognized as a major trading port in the world, and because of that, everyone who was anyone in the world wanted a piece of it. But on July 9, 1776, at the start of the American Revolution—when much of Manhattan was yet a field—New York declared its independence from Britain and became one of the thirteen original colonies, and in 1783, the British finally ceded New York City to the colonies for good. In 1789, George Washington was inaugurated as the first president of the United States at Federal Hall on Wall Street, and New York City served as the capital of the fledgling nation until the following year.

By 1835, New York had become the largest city in the United States, a distinction it maintains to this day, thanks in large part to the masses of immigrants who have settled here. Since 1886, immigrants, visitors, and those returning to the New York Harbor have been greeted by the colossal Statue of Liberty on Liberty Island. A gift from the French, Lady Liberty, as she is called, beckons all newcomers with Emma Lazarus's 1903 poem inscribed in a bronze plaque on the base of the statue that says, in part, "Give me your tired, your poor, your huddled masses yearning to breathe free." And so they came. This was, after all, the land of freedom and opportunity. But what is it *today* that draws people to the Big Apple, as it is affectionately called? Simple. The city is a world leader in culture, with Broadway, the Lincoln Center for Performing Arts, and its many museums; in finance, with the New York Stock Exchange and NASDAQ; and in politics, with the United Nations headquarters located in Manhattan. It's a major center of transportation, religion, higher education, commerce, industry, the media, the arts, and real estate.

In 1898, the city's current boundaries were set, encompassing five distinct and adjacent regions that, when consolidated, became the five boroughs that make up New York City. Today, each borough is synonymous with a specific county: the Bronx is Bronx County, Brooklyn is Kings County, Manhattan is New York County, Queens is Queens County, and Staten Island is Richmond County. Each has its own unique haunted history and unforgettable stories of ghosts and other phenomena.

The Bronx

THE BOROUGH KNOWN AS THE BRONX REFERS TO THE BRONX RIVER, which was named after Swedish sea captain Jonas Bronck, who established a farm along the Harlem River around 1639. Out of the five New York City boroughs, the Bronx is the fourth most populated, with 1.3 million residents. It is the northernmost borough and the only one located primarily on the mainland, rather than on an island. During Prohibition, the Bronx was infested with bootleggers and speakeasies, which contributed to increased crime and street gangs, and that poor urban image has been perpetuated by the media in films like *Fort Apache, the Bronx*. But regardless of the sometimes tarnished image of some of its neighborhoods, the Bronx as a whole holds many gems of New York City, including Yankee Stadium, the New York Botanical Gardens, and the Bronx Zoo, where you can see every animal imaginable, to the tune of more than four thousand—but don't expect to see that elusive enigma, the unicorn. They haven't been seen in the Bronx since the 1600s. Nor will you find the man-owl-tiger beast that the zoo was solicited to capture in 1904.

Pelham Bay is one of the borough's more upscale areas, even though it's historically been considered one of the most haunted neighborhoods in the Bronx, especially near Cedar Knoll, where headless Indians and phantom pirates are said to roam. And in nearby Pelham, an elegant—though forgetful—old woman still searches for the gold she hid in her own house to prevent it from being stolen by others. Fordham University is believed to have a mattress-flipping ghost and a phantom Jesuit priest in hot pursuit of it. The Bronx also has inexplicable phenomena of a seemingly divine nature at its Lourdes of America grotto and at Joseph Vitolo's shrine to the Virgin Mary just south of Van Cortlandt Park.

Fordham University

St. John's Hall, the earliest part of Fordham University, was built as the archdiocesan seminary in 1844 and became part of St. John's College in 1860, when it was combined with St. Robert's and Bishop's Halls. Today these three buildings form Queen's Court, a first-year residential college . . . and the most haunted place on campus.

In the summer of 2003, the only people occupying Queen's Court were five resident assistants (RAs) and a residence director (RD) for each hall. Their task was to complete condition reports on each room of outgoing freshmen and prepare the rooms for incoming freshmen. In one room on the first floor of St. Robert's wing, which was built in 1940, something strange began happening to the mattresses. Each time an RA entered the room, they found the mattresses of both beds leaning upright against the wall. At first the RA assumed it was one of the other RAs playing a practical joke. But nobody came forward. Finally, one of the RAs came up with the idea to lock that room's door after making sure the mattresses were lying on the beds where they should be. That would keep the pranksters away, assuming they didn't have access to the key. An hour later, the RA returned to the room and was startled to find the mattresses leaning against the wall again—in the securely locked room.

Later that night, things got even weirder. The same RA who had locked the door in a futile attempt to stop what he thought was a prankster was awakened by a knock at the door. It was a Jesuit priest—the order that runs Fordham University—and he told the RA that "it," meaning a mischievous ghost, usually stayed in a room at the end of the hall but had gotten out. The priest told the young man that there was nothing to worry about—he had "taken care of it." The next morning, the RA went to the office of the head nun to thank her for dispatching the priest, because he assumed she had spoken to the priest about the mattress pranks and requested assistance, since by then everyone on campus was aware of the strange situation. The nun said, however, that not only had she never seen a priest that fit the late-night visitor's description, but as far as she knew, nobody on campus had asked a priest to pay the RA a visit. Was the Jesuit priest who came to the rescue a ghost who was eternally trying to keep another ghost in line? Was the whole mattress incident an elaborate and lengthy practical joke, or was it really a genuine ghost story from a haunted university?

Besides the mattress-flipping phantom, there's a tale told about a Jesuit priest who allegedly hanged himself in a dorm hallway and was found dead with his dangling feet swaying back and forth, bumping against the radiator. According to the RAs and RDs, who love to spook the incoming freshmen with ghost stories, that's why the radiator often makes a repetitive thumping noise to this day. There are plenty of ghost stories from all around Fordham University, usually involving young children who don't belong on campus. From Finley Hall come reports of doors slamming shut inexplicably, furniture being moved by unseen hands, and the sound of a child's laughter. Apparitions of children have been witnessed by students at Hughes Hall and in the dorm at Martyr's Court, where a terrified student once reported seeing a young girl standing silently in a shower looking straight ahead.

Lourdes of America

In 1932, Monsignor Pasquale Lombardo, the founder of St. Lucy's Roman Catholic Church, visited the site of Lourdes, France, where it is said that the Virgin Mary appeared to a young girl in the nineteenth century. A shrine was constructed at the sacred Lourdes site, where a healing spring that bubbled through the rocks was believed to be responsible for many miracles. Father Lombardo made it his mission to re-create that shrine in the Bronx as a place of prayer and hope for the faithful. In 1939, he opened his Lourdes of America at the Church of St. Lucy at 833 Mace Avenue, complete with a four-foot statue of the Virgin Mary perched atop a man-made spring where "miracle water" cascades over the rocks, just as in Lourdes. It doesn't matter to the devout that the water from the spring is simply tapped from the New York City water lines; their faith, belief, and prayers are enough to cause numerous reported healings at the location in the Bronx, and it's been happening since the day Lourdes of America first opened.

According to *Time* magazine's July 24, 1939, issue, in an article called "Miracle in the Bronx," a Mrs. Anthony Geraci hobbled to the shrine's pool, dragging her left foot in a steel brace. Like many others, she sipped the water and prayed. When she felt a sudden prickling on her paralyzed limb, she slipped off the shoe and brace and stood in the pool. That's when her miracle occurred. She stepped out of the water, jumped up and down on two suddenly healthy feet, and *ran* the ten blocks to her home to show her husband. The miracle caused such excitement that the police had to be called in for crowd control. Other remarkable cures and healings became a normal occurrence over the years, such as people who were healed just before surgery or after battling long illnesses. Then, in 2001, it happened again: another miracle. A woman who had been using crutches since a disabling accident in 2000 visited the shrine, and when she left, she was walking without crutches for the first time.

The Archdiocese of New York has never investigated the grotto for its claims of divine healing powers, but the believers and the healed don't need a nod of approval from the church to trust that the site is sacred and miraculous.

The Bronx Miracle

Joseph Vitolo Jr. was a slight nine-year-old boy, the eighteenth child of poor Italian immigrants, when he first encountered the Virgin Mary in the Bronx. It happened near his home just south of Van Cortlandt Park on October 29, 1945. According to an article in the November 26, 1945, *Time* magazine called "Shrine in the Bronx," the Holy Mother told Vitolo to pray and promised to return for sixteen nights. The boy told his family and friends, and they accompanied him the following night, when he again saw the vision, though he was the only one who could. Nevertheless, word quickly spread throughout the community and the nation. The second night that Vitolo returned to the site of his encounter, as instructed by the Blessed Mother, he was accompanied by about two hundred people, and by the sixteenth night, the crowd had grown to an astonishing thirty thousand. That's how fast word of the "miracle in the Bronx" spread . . . pretty impressive for a pre-Internet world.

People came hoping to see a miracle in action or be healed by the touch of the blessed young boy. For along with the obvious gift of communication with a divine being, Vitolo had developed a gift of healing. Some who came to see the "chosen one" (Vitolo) were healed by the boy's touch and prayers, such as a baby with a paralyzed hand that was suddenly healed after being pressed into the soil from the site of the Virgin Mary apparitions. Vitolo also allegedly healed his own father. After placing his hand on his doubtful father's aching back, which had kept the man idle, the pain vanished, and the senior Vitolo was able to return to work.

Even the rich and famous were impressed with the child's curative abilities. Frank Sinatra gifted the boy with a large statue of the Virgin Mary, which Vitolo keeps in his living room to this day, and Lou Costello of Abbott and Costello fame sent the boy a glass-enclosed figurine. The cardinal and his entourage even paid the young Vitolo a visit. Yet the Archdiocese of New York still refused to confirm the validity of the miracles occurring in their own backyard, as often seems to be the case in similar situations. Nevertheless, the public embraced the notion of the Blessed Virgin Mary in the Bronx, and magazine giants like *Time* and *Life* found the phenomenon sensational enough to devote entire articles to it.

For a young boy of nine and his large family of modest means, the sudden fame must have been overwhelming. But the publicity diminished rapidly after Vitolo's final encounter with the Virgin Mary. Still, over the years, the faithful have continued to visit the site. Today most people are unaware of the Bronx miracle, but Joseph Vitolo never wavered in his belief of what he saw and experienced as a youngster, even when some people called him a crackpot. He was never a fan of publicity, and he never made money from his experiences, so what purpose could concocting such a story possibly serve?

Instead, Vitolo has continued to honor the Holy Mother and the miracles he experienced, still living in his childhood home near the shrine he built at the exact location of his encounters with the Virgin Mary so many years ago. Nearly every night of his life since 1945, he has climbed the hill behind his house to recite the Rosary at the shrine.

Cedar Knoll's Headless Tribe

Cedar Knoll is located in a remote section of Pelham Bay Park on Shoal Harbor and is not easily accessible to the public, but that may not be a bad thing, since the sight of headless phantom warriors isn't what I would call suitable for general audiences. For it was there on Cedar Knoll overlooking Long Island Sound that a fierce battle between Long Island's Matinecock tribe and Shoal Harbor's Siwanoy tribe in the mid-1600s resulted in the defeat of the latter, when the entire tribe was decapitated on its own turf. Since that time, reports of phantom Indians carrying their heads in their hands and chanting eerily around the site have contributed to the nickname of "Haunted Cedar Knoll."

The sheer volume of genuine arrowheads unearthed at the knoll substantiates the legends of the land being a battleground, and archaeologists believe the arrowheads may have actually been manufactured on-site prior to that bloody battle. In 1881, Westchester County historian Robert Bolton Jr. said of the legendary ghosts of Cedar Knoll that "the forms of many headless Indians might be seen on moonlit nights, in a circle, performing a kind of war dance on its summit with heads in their hands." It was likely that a "severe and sanguinary battle had taken place" there, he said, resulting in the decapitation of an entire tribe—and perhaps a subsequent headless ghost tribe. But Cedar Knoll is not the Pelham area's only claim to fame in the paranormal arena.

Parrish House

Alexander Diack built the old stone house at 463 First Avenue in the village of Pelham in 1851 and sold it to James Parrish unfinished in 1855. Since then, the home, modeled after a Scottish townhouse of one of Diack's ancestors, has been referred to as both the Parrish House and the Old Stone House. Mr. Parrish came into hard-earned wealth after joining forces with an employee of his, a man named Adams, and operating a successful "express business," a private mail delivery service that provided an alternative to the post office. After Parrish's death, his widow continued receiving his share of dividends in the form of gold coins from the surviving business partner.

Legend has it that after being robbed at the Parrish homestead by masked men, the clever, if forgetful, Mrs. Parrish began to hide her gold—and very well, I might add—in various locations throughout the old stone house to ensure greater difficulty for any other thief inclined to steal from her. The problem is that she hid her gold so well that even *she* couldn't remember where she hid it. At the time of her death, it was believed that some of her gold was still unaccounted for. And since then, people have reported seeing an apparition of the elegant woman, dressed in her best, as she always was, wandering through the house as if still searching for the rest of her misplaced fortune.

In a 1946 book with a very long title called *A Brief, but Most Complete & True Account of the Settlement of the Ancient Town of Pelham Westchester County, State of New York, Known One Time Well & Favourably as the Lordship & Manor of Pelham*, Lockwood Anderson Barr writes: "It is said that a million dollars in gold is hidden in the house, or buried in the gardens. Search has been made of the house, and grounds excavated, but without result. However, underneath a hearthstone in the basement kitchen, a hundred small coins of early date were found by one of the owners—but no pot of gold."

In her last days, Mrs. Parrish resided with a Wm. H. Sparks, and she bequeathed her house to him for his kindness. Later, the Old Stone House passed through the hands of many others, including an architect named Francis Miles Snyder in 1920, who restored the home. Today, the privately owned Pelham landmark remains as attractive—and its history as intriguing—as ever.

The Fire Ship

While Cedar Knoll has its phantom headless tribe, Long Island Sound in the Pelham and New Rochelle vicinity boasts a phantom "Fire Ship." According to local lore, in the mid-seventeenth century, back in the dangerous days of Captain Kidd, pirates took over a ship and killed the crew. Though a single white horse was spared the horrific fate of the crew, it soon met a fate even crueler, as it slowly, agonizingly succumbed in the flames of a fire set by the pirates.

It is said to this day, during violent thunderstorms, Pelham's "Fire Ship" sometimes returns from its watery grave and can be seen rushing through the water, aglow in flames, with a spectral crew of the "undead" manning their posts. The horse, eternally spooked, is rearing and bucking, frantic to escape its hellish grave.

The Hoodoo Post

Where have all the man-owl-tiger beasts gone? In the late 1800s and early 1900s, there were an unusually large number of reports of unidentified, malevolent creatures flying across New York City and the New England states. Provincetown, Massachusetts, was terrorized by a creature called Jumping Black Flash, described in detail in *Haunted Massachusetts: Ghosts and Strange Phenomena of the Bay State*. This darkly cloaked, supernatural being jumped onto rooftops and down from trees, taunting people with an evil grin and spraying them with blue flames from its gaping mouth. After attempts by law enforcement to capture the beast, it was the quick, fearless wit of a few determined children that scared it away for good. But a strikingly similar creature was reported in England shortly after. The English dubbed their flying menace Spring-Heeled Jack. In another section of this book, I describe sightings of a bat-like man flying over Coney Island and Brooklyn, heading due east. He too was darkly clothed (or skinned) and sported an evil grin.

In 1904, the *New York Times* ran an article about a flying creature that was attacking residents and police officers of the Bronx Park Police Station, Post 16, on Lorillard Lane. Some who saw the hideous creature described it as a winged, man-size demon; others called it a "wildcat with wings" because it screamed like a tiger. Those who didn't see it at all said it must have been simply a large owl. I'll call it a man-owl-tiger beast to cover all descriptions. Whatever it was, so many police officers saw the flying enigma that Post 16 became known as the "hoodoo post," a term that aptly described the disturbing supernatural misfortune the post was enduring.

Several officers were so shaken by their experiences with the being that they had to be transferred to other posts. One officer saw the creature closely enough to hear it growl and establish that it definitely was not an owl. Another officer who saw the thing said it had to be supernatural, because it tried to hit him in the head with a stick clutched in its giant claws. The officer assigned to replace him didn't fare any better, having the creature knock his helmet off his head. Yet another officer was attacked by what he called "a dark flying object with four legs and two wings." He said in the police report he filed that the creature alternately took the form of a "tall slim man" and a "mountain dwarf." A shapeshifter? A giant owl gone mad? The police chief requested the assistance of the Zoological Garden's superintendent to capture what he stubbornly believed to be a large (albeit man-eating) brown owl.

No further stories were ever published on that particular subject, so whatever it was, it eluded capture—as creatures of cryptozoology inevitably do. (Cryptozoology is the study of creatures whose existence has not been proven.) It's been a long time since anything like Coney Island's man-owl-tiger beast has been reported in the New York City area, or anywhere, for that matter.

Unicorns in the Bronx

A long time ago when the earth was green, there were more kinds of animals than you've ever seen. Cats and rats and elephants as sure as you're born, but the loveliest of all was the unicorn . . .
—"The Unicorn Song" by poet/songwriter Shel Silverstein

Well, the earth *was* pretty green in the 1600s, when influential Dutch immigrants like Adriaen Van der Donck were settling the primitive land of New Amsterdam. Van der Donck, for whom the neighboring city of Yonkers was named, was the first lawyer of the early Dutch colony and a prominent political leader of the time. He was also well respected by the native tribes of the region, from whom he gleaned much information about the new land he was so instrumental in settling. In fact, today he is recognized as "a sympathetic early Native American ethnographer, having learned the languages and observed the customs of the Mahicans and Mohawks," according to the online encyclopedia *Wikipedia.* As fate would have it, the noble Dutchman was also a very articulate author who put his vast knowledge to good use in a comprehensive piece considered by scholars and historians to be the most complete and accurate account of New Netherland ever written.

Van der Donck's *A Description of the New Netherlands* includes exceptional portrayals of the land and its endless resources and possibilities, as well as of the Indians who first inhabited it and their interactions with the earliest settlers. The cover page of the document says it describes "the fruitfulness and natural advantage of the country, and the desirable opportunities which it presents, within itself, and from abroad, for the subsistence of man; which are not surpassed elsewhere. Together with remarks on the character and peculiar customs of the savages, or natives of the land."

Van der Donck's decisive book describes in great detail the natural resources of the land, including vegetation and animals. One such animal appears to have been the *unicorn*:

> I have also been frequently told by the Mohawk Indians, that far in the interior parts of the country, there were animals which were seldom seen, of the size and form of horses, with cloven hoofs, having one horn in the forehead, from a foot and a half to two feet in length, and that because of their fleetness and strength they were seldom caught or ensnared. I have never seen any certain token or sign of such animals, but that such creatures exist in the country, is supported by the concurrent declarations of the Indian hunters. There are Christians who say that they have seen the skins of this species of animal, but without the horns.

In 1809, Washington Irving, under the pseudonym of Diedrich Knickerbocker, wrote about unicorns in his satirical piece called *A History of New York, from the Beginning of the World to the End of the Dutch Dynasty*, Vol. 1.

> Let. of I. Megapol. Hag. S. P. Ogilvie, in his excellent account of America, speaking of these parts, makes mention of Lions, which abounded on a high mountain, and likewise observes, "On the borders of Canada there is seen sometimes a kind of beast which hath some resemblance with a horse, having cloven feet, shaggy mane, one horn just on the forehead, a tail like that of a wild hog, and a deer's neck." He furthermore gives a picture of this strange beast, which resembles exceedingly an unicorn. It is much to be lamented by philosophers, that this miraculous breed of animals, like that of a horned frog, is totally extinct.

Whether unicorns have existed ever is a matter of speculation, for much like Bigfoot and the Loch Ness Monster, no unicorn has ever been captured that we are currently aware of. Some believe the mystical creature did exist at one time but is now extinct; others believe unicorns are pure fantasy; and still others believe they exist but can be found only in the farthest regions of the earth by those possessing extraordinary honesty and virtue. Whatever the case may be, unicorns reportedly have been sighted at least since the time of Adam and Eve in their Garden of Eden, but there have been few documented sightings in the last four thousand years. The Chinese may have an explanation for that. In their mythology, a unicorn's appearance was considered a good omen, a sign of good times, and something of utmost importance was always implied. For example, five millennia ago, Emperor Fu Hsi was said to have received the secrets of written language by a unicorn. In 551 B.C., another story has it, a pregnant Chinese woman was approached by a unicorn in the woods and presented with an inscribed piece of jade. When the animal laid its head in her lap, she knew it was a good omen. She gave birth to the great philosopher Confucius shortly after, and just as the inscription had predicted, Confucius was indeed possessed of great wisdom. The philosopher himself saw the unicorn in his old age and knew it meant his time here was nearly complete. Other famous people who said they encountered unicorns were Alexander the Great, Julius Caesar, and Genghis Khan.

Who knows? Maybe when goodness and prosperity rule across our planet, or another monumental moment in history is afoot, as the ancient Chinese believed, someone among us will be approached by the mythical creature, and the age-old question of its authenticity will finally be answered.

Brooklyn

THE VILLAGE OF BROOKLYN WAS FOUNDED IN 1646 BY THE DUTCH, WHO named it after a Dutch city called "Breuckelen." As with the rest of New York, the Dutch lost Brooklyn to the British in 1664, and then the British lost Brooklyn when the colonies gained their independence in the Revolutionary War. In fact, the first major—and what would be the largest—battle in the war was fought in late summer 1776 in Kings County (conterminous with Brooklyn). Today Brooklyn is the most populous borough in New York City, with almost 2.5 million residents, and Kings County is New York State's most populated county. Brooklyn is on the westernmost point of Long Island, bounded by the borough of Queens to the northeast.

After the arrival of rail service in the 1870s, Brooklyn's population surged with upwardly mobile immigrants of diverse ethnic backgrounds moving in from more expensive (and congested) areas like Manhattan, which is why today you see signs around Brooklyn that appropriately call the borough "Home to Everyone from Everywhere!" Coney Island became a popular district on the Atlantic Ocean, a "Playground by the Sea" for the rich and famous in the late 1800s and early 1900s. And it was about this time that a strange, black creature appearing to be half man and half something that was definitely *not* man was reportedly seen flying over Coney Island, prompting a media frenzy. If it was a clever publicity stunt to lure more thrill seekers to what was then America's largest amusement park, it didn't hurt. But when subways were introduced as an economical mode of travel in the 1920s, Coney Island became easily accessible to everyone, regardless of financial status, and its amusement park became wildly popular, attracting up to a million visitors a day during its heyday in the 1950s—even without its mysterious black flying creature.

Coney Island isn't the only place you'll find excitement—or supernatural beings—in Brooklyn; they have been reported from all over the borough.

Stuyvesant Heights definitely loved its bell-ringing ghost of yesteryear, and in 1892, hundreds were attracted to the demolition of a home on Moore Street where a young boy and his mother had been murdered, because they were certain the alleged child ghost would make his final appearance when the tenement was razed. Most Holy Trinity Church on Montrose and Graham has such popular ghost stories that the church now devotes an entire page to them on its website. And ghosts allegedly have haunted a historic brewery on Liberty Avenue, a fabled mansion in the Flatbush neighborhood, and a sidewalk on Union Street, not to mention the paranormal phenomena still reported at the McCarren Park Pool in the Greenpoint section of Brooklyn. If the mounds of archived newspaper articles reporting supernatural phenomena are any indication, you don't have to go far to find a place with a haunted history in this "borough of homes and churches."

The Bellringer

In the early 1900s, guides conducting tours through Stuyvesant Heights were instructed to point out 281 Stuyvesant Avenue as the neighborhood's "genuine haunted house," and the guides were happy to oblige. If you think ghosts and the paranormal are hot topics today, you should have been around in the 1800s and early 1900s when every week, it seems, another haunted house or building was making the news. All the other neighborhoods in the city were talking about *their* ghosts, and Stuyvesant Heights was not about to be outdone. But the Griffins, the ones having to deal with the ghost, didn't share their neighbors' enthusiasm, so they moved to Bedford Avenue, leaving their friendly ghost behind.

They had lived on the first floor of the apartment building at 281 Stuyvesant Avenue, an address that today is home to the

Mocada Cultural Center, the Bridge Street Headstart, and the Bridge Street AME Church. At the time the Griffins lived there, Stuyvesant Heights was an area of brownstones, two-story homes, and churches. The Griffins' apartment house was adjacent to Grace Presbyterian Church. According to a *Brooklyn Daily Eagle* article dated October 23, 1901, the ghost "began by ringing the electric bell in the vestibule promptly at 2 o'clock every afternoon . . . with the fiendish persistency of a book agent." The paranormal phenomena experienced by the couple included the usual "hollow groans, creepy sidesteps on the staircases, and unexpected trips from room to room by articles of furniture." The newlyweds hastily moved out—not because they were afraid, they insisted, but because the constant disturbances were simply too annoying. And if you want to believe that, I've got a bridge in Brooklyn to sell you . . .

Most Holy Trinity Church

Father John Stephen Raffeiner was born to a pious, wealthy family in Austria the day after Christmas 1785. Though he had been a physician in the Napoleonic Wars, in 1825 he was ordained to the priesthood. Then he received word from the States that priests were needed to minister to the growing German immigrant population in the Brooklyn area. Father Raffeiner, who had made a small fortune as a physician, used his wealth to establish St. Nicholas Parish— the oldest German church in the New York diocese—in 1836 and the Most Holy Trinity Roman Catholic Church in 1841. The first Trinity Church was a simple frame building on Montrose Avenue, where Father Raffeiner lived in the basement.

After the Reverend John Raufeisen succeeded Raffeiner in 1850, a larger church with two majestic towers was built to accommodate the growing congregation. The site chosen, at the corner of Montrose and Graham Avenues, had been a parochial burial ground. The remains of those buried there were transferred to a lot adjacent to the Evergreen Cemetery. Today the parish school building, circa 1877, is on the site. And legend has it that not all of the bodies were transferred from the original burial ground, even though their headstones were, leading many people to believe that there are restless souls still wandering about searching for their tombstones. Their suspicions are further supported by lights in the school gym going on and off inexplicably, and voices and footsteps often heard by janitorial staff at night when nobody else is around.

With the ever-increasing Catholic population in the parish, a third and final, much larger church was built, and it held its first service in 1882. This is the Holy Trinity Church you see today—the one said to be haunted. The church claims that because of so many queries regarding the legends of its ghosts, it decided to share the most popular ghost stories on its website, "solely for entertainment purposes," of course. According to the website, the secret passageways, false closets, and tunnels known to exist on the triforium level of the church were used for runaway slaves from the South, escaping to freedom in the North via the Underground Railroad. Two of the church's early pastors, Raffeiner and May, are buried in the crypt beneath the church. The latter pastor died in his sleep in his room on the second floor in 1895. Today, May's bedroom is believed haunted by some who have slept there in its capacity as a guest room. The sounds of someone pacing the floor, as well as other strange noises, have been heard. Loud, distinctive footsteps have been heard on the rectory staircase in the middle of the night, and dogs have reacted to something unseen on the stairs that lead to the basement.

In 1897, a parish sexton and bellringer named George Stelz was murdered in the church vestibule. Although there was a prime suspect in the case, he escaped conviction, so the murder was considered unsolved—which would certainly qualify as "unfinished business" to a ghost. Stelz's blood, the legend goes, continues to appear on the wall in the stairway leading to the bell tower. His spirit is believed to still roam the building, ringing the bell for attention, and it may continue to do so until his murderer is properly accused. Better posthumously than never.

Union Street Ghost

"All in White—A Pretty Young Ghost Haunting South Brooklyn." That was the headline of the first in a series of newspaper articles the *Brooklyn Daily Eagle* ran more than a hundred years ago regarding what would become known as the Union Street Ghost. On August 12, 1890, the *Eagle* ran a report about the supernatural encounter of a patrolman named Thomas McGrath in what was then the Eleventh Precinct:

Brooklyn

At 3:15 o'clock last Saturday morning, I was patrolling Union Street, near the corner of Columbia . . . I saw a woman passing along in front of the jewelry store on the south side. I thought it was strange that a woman should be out at that time in the morning and walked toward her. I was then distant about 100 feet . . . She walked along Columbia . . . I crossed Union Street with the intention of meeting her . . . We approached to within ten feet of each other and were coming still closer when the woman completely disappeared. I was going toward her. I had my eye on her and there was nothing between us, and the electric light was shining full on her when she disappeared.

Officer McGrath went on to describe the apparition as being young—perhaps about eighteen years old—and very pretty. She was dressed in white from head to toe, wearing "a Mother Hubbard gown and a Nellie Bly hat." "She moved very slowly and her footsteps made no sound," he said, and her gown didn't flow the way he was used to seeing women's gowns flow as they walked. The experience shook him to the core. The poor man insisted that what he described was the solid truth and that he'd rather not have it printed in newspapers for fear of public ridicule. He didn't believe in ghosts until he saw one himself, saying, "I would have laughed at a man a week ago who talked of ghosts to me, but I know better now." As if he hadn't been traumatized enough by his encounter, his fear of public ridicule was realized when he became the butt of jokes by the mixed population of immigrants in his South Brooklyn neighborhood.

But the laughter stopped when other credible witnesses came forward with their stories. A sixteen-year-old stable boy and his little brother were awakened by the stifling heat on the night of the alleged incident, looked out their window, and saw "a woman in white standing on the edge of the curb stone on the northeast corner of Union and Columbia Streets." The stable boy said he watched as the patrolman approached her, and then went back to bed, not thinking anything of it; he hadn't watched long enough to see the woman vanish into thin air. It wasn't until early the next morning when he went to work that he heard about the patrolman and the ghost lady. The boy's description of the woman matched the patrolman's: "She moved very slowly and held her hands clasped in front of her and hanging down at their full length. She was standing quite still when I saw her first, but began to move about shortly afterward. She was dressed in white from head to foot and had a sort of white hood over her head."

The watchman whom the patrolman first spoke to regarding the young woman said he had seen the same woman shortly before 3 A.M. coming out of 84 Union Street. He said it looked like an Italian woman dressed in white. After hearing the patrolman's story, he recalled the murder of an Italian bride on her wedding night seven years earlier . . . at that very address, 84 Union Street.

McCarren Park Pool

In 2006, an outdoor entertainment promoter under the direction of media giant Clear Channel began staging concerts at the abandoned McCarren Park Pool in the bordering Greenpoint district. McCarren Pool was one of eleven giant pools (three times the size of an Olympic pool, with a capacity of sixty-eight hundred) built by the Works Progress Administration (WPA) during the Depression in 1936. Then-mayor LaGuardia said in opening-day ceremonies, "No pool anywhere has been as much appreciated as this one."

As anticipated, for many years the pool was the hub of summertime activity in that neighborhood. Then in 1979, New York City approved $100 million to restore all of its public pools in time for the fiftieth anniversary of the pools in 1986. The McCarren Park Pool was closed in 1984 to begin repairs, and a razor-wire fence secured the ground. But the community was concerned that restoring the pool at McCarren Park would only attract undesirables and crime to the neighborhood, so the planned restoration at that time never took place, and the pool never reopened—at least not as a pool. McCarren Park Pool became a public eyesore in the neighborhood, a concrete wasteland of graffiti, broken glass, and rusty razor wire.

Today, McCarren Park Pool is a historic cultural landmark that was resurrected as a spectacular venue for outdoor concerts in 2006. As such, it's difficult to imagine that it is possibly haunted, yet that's what they say. Allegedly, a tragedy once occurred at McCarren Park when a little girl drowned in the pool. Since then, rumors have run rampant that her spirit roams around the park—specifically in the pool area itself—calling for help. I don't know that anyone has reported seeing or hearing a ghost in quite some time there, but according to the Paranormal Investigation of NYC website, there was

Palisades Park Public Library
257 2nd St/(201)585-4150
palisadespark.bccls.org
Encouraging a lifetime
love of learning

Title: Haunted New York City :
ghosts and strange phenom

Item ID: 39153090543150
Call number: 133.109 REV
Date due: 8/5/2010,23:59

Title: Space clearing A-Z : how
to use Feng Shui to puri
Item ID: 39153090218712
Call number: 133.33 LINN
Date due: 8/5/2010,23:59

Title: Lillian Too's irresistible
feng shui magic : 48 s
Item ID: 39153090218134
Call number: 133.333 TOO
Date due: 8/5/2010,23:59

Mon-Thu: 10:30am - 9pm
Fri: 10:30am - 5pm
Sat: 10:30am - 4pm
Closed Wkends in July & August

some evidence of spirit activity when they investigated the site from the outside perimeter of the fenced complex before it was converted into a concert venue. They reported picking up anomalous EMF readings and discovering cold spots with marked temperature drops, both believed to sometimes indicate the presence of spirit energy.

So you may want to bring along a sweater if you go to a concert at McCarren Park Pool. You never know who—or what—you will bump into.

Fortune-Telling of Yesteryear

"Born with natural gift; she tells past, present, and future; she brings together those long separated . . . shows you a correct likeness of your future husband or friends in love affairs. She was never known to fail. Two thousand dollars reward for anyone that can equal her in professional skill. Ladies fifty cents to one dollar. Positively no gents admitted."

You'd never get a clairvoyant reading for fifty cents today—the going rate is more like fifty *dollars*. But that ad was an example of the type often seen in city journals of nineteenth-century New York, according to author Edward Winslow Martin (aka James Dabney McCabe), in his 1868 publication, *The Secrets of the Great City: A Work Descriptive of the Virtues and Vices, the Mysteries, Miseries, and Crimes of New York City.* "It seems strange that, in this boasted age of enlightenment, the persons who make such announcements as the above can find anyone simple enough to believe them," said Martin. "Yet, it is a fact, that these persons . . . make large sums of money out of the credulity of their fellow creatures."

Today, fortune telling is a multimillion-dollar industry, thanks primarily to the Internet. Now anyone with a credit card has easy access to his or her own personal psychic at any time. Regardless of what skeptics of yesteryear, like Martin, have to say about clairvoyance, modern society embraces the whole spectrum of psychic abilities, including spirit channeling, clairvoyancy, and fortune-telling. We're awed by the great psychics of the day. Sylvia Browne, John Edward, and James Van Praagh are all best-selling authors and TV personalities because of the public's unquenchable thirst for the information they can glean. We *want* to believe that *someone* has all the answers for us and can tell us if something good (or even bad) is in our future. We want to believe that our deceased loved ones are waiting for the opportunity to speak to us from beyond, mainly for reassurance that they're okay on the other side. That's human nature. So there will always be people seeking out those with the ability to connect us with the other side, those who can divine our future. But we've come a long way since the days of fifty-cent readings and dark rooms with crystal balls.

Yet today we're as susceptible to being duped as we were a hundred years ago. Though there are some genuinely gifted psychics, there are also many phonies, and the only thing they can sense is the sweet smell of cash in the pocket of a vulnerable individual. The New York Penal Law, Section 165.35—Fortune-Telling, as antiquated as it is, certainly hasn't slowed them down any. According to that law, which doesn't leave room for the possibility that some psychics and fortune-tellers are legitimate:

> A person is guilty of fortune-telling when, for a fee or compensation which he directly or indirectly solicits or receives, he claims or pretends to tell fortunes, or holds himself out as being able, by claimed or pretended use of occult powers, to answer questions or give advice on personal matters or to exorcise, influence, or affect evil spirits or curses; except that this section does not apply to a person who engages in the afore-described conduct as part of a show or exhibition solely for the purpose of entertainment or amusement. Fortune-telling is a class B misdemeanor.

The law today is reserved for cases of obvious swindling, which is difficult to prove with psychic phenomenon, but it wasn't uncommon a century ago to have busts in which fortune-tellers around New York City were corralled and arrested for their "crime," as in the example below.

An article titled "The Sin of Telling Fortunes" in the June 20, 1897, *Brooklyn Eagle* tells of a Brooklyn man who claimed to be an "Eastern Mystic," selling fortunes for $3 to a detective who worked for the district attorney's office. The man was arrested (bet he didn't see *that* coming) after telling the detective that if she paid him more than $3, he could "have told a better fortune . . . and could have gotten her married to the dark young man . . . while for $17 more, he could likewise have made her mother inherit some property." The *Eagle* reporter, clearly not a fan of psychics, summed up his thoughts by saying the alleged Eastern Mystic's "place is in the fourteenth century, and it is feared that he will have hard work to catch up with that." Like I said, we really have come a long way.

Melrose Hall

On the corner of Winthrop Street and Bedford Avenue in the Flatbush District once stood a historic and long-haunted mansion called Melrose Hall, for the park it was located in. The house was built by an Englishman named Lane in 1749. It was three stories high with countless windows and gables in every direction. The interior was handsomely elegant, with oak paneling, gilded cornices, a ballroom, library, large foyer, and elaborate garden terraces. Those were only the noticeable features. Hidden from general view were the secret staircases, passageways, and concealed rooms.

Upon Lane's death, which occurred shortly after he built the mansion, the property passed to Colonel William Axtell, known as "William the Gay" as a youth for his carefree demeanor. Axtell and his wife, Margaret DePeyster, were prominent both politically and socially on the New York City circuit, with a mansion on Broadway and their Melrose Hall. Axtell, who would become a key player in the ghost story associated with Melrose Hall, was at first favorable to the Colonial party at the start of the Revolution, but in 1776, he changed his views and took sides with the Mother Country, becoming a colonel and commander to a loyalist regiment known as the Nassau Blues. The infamous Blues were feared for the torture they inflicted on rebel prisoners who embraced the patriot cause. The alleged torture took place at Melrose Hall, even as lavish parties for the loyalist elite were being hosted there. (So much for William's gaiety.) Because of its identification as a torture chamber, the U.S. government placed Melrose Hall high on its list of estates to confiscated under the New York Act of Attainder of 1779.

Colonel Axtell and his wife had no children of their own but adopted Elizabeth Shipton, who ended up marrying a man Axtell despised because of their different political stands. Ironically, that man, Colonel Aquila Giles of the Continental Army, bought Melrose Mansion after the property was seized by the government and sold in 1784. Giles formerly had been forbidden to return to the property where his future wife lived, but that all changed when he became the new owner. Elizabeth and Colonel Giles lived there happily for twenty-five years. Axtell died in England in 1795, but some of the legends propagated by the media had him dying of mysterious causes associated with an illicit love affair he had during his tenure at Melrose Hall. After Giles moved out, Melrose Hall passed through the hands of many people, starting with Bateman Lloyd, who died of natural causes at the mansion. After Lloyd's heirs moved on, a famous actress who was also an author and playwright, Anna Cora Mowatt, moved in with her husband, James, who was a lawyer. Mrs. Mowatt earned her fame by her own determined efforts and sheer talent after James lost their entire fortune in stocks. In 1854, she wrote of her five happy years at Melrose Hall in *Autobiography of an Actress*, saying:

> There were dark and spacious vaults beneath the kitchens, where it was said English prisoners had been confined; and there was a secret chamber above the great ballroom to which no access could be found, save by a small window. The neighbors affirmed that a young girl had been purposely starved to death in that chamber and that her ghost wandered at night about the house. Indeed, this report had gained such credence that nothing could have induced many of the elder inhabitants of the village to pass a night beneath the haunted roof.

Regardless of its lurid past, Mrs. Mowatt was very fond of Melrose Hall and said they "gave the place the name of Melrose not from any likeness to Melrose Abbey, but on account of the abundance of roses of every description which grew about the place in wonderful luxuriance." After the Mowatts moved out of Melrose, it went through a series of owners: Dudley Sheldon, Dr. John Robinson, Mrs. John Metcalfe, Dr. Bartlett, the Rev. Drowne, and Dr. T. S. Drowne. When Dr. Drowne passed away, his wife put the property up for sale. After a six-year period of vacancy, Charles Salter purchased Melrose Hall in 1901 for just $5,700 at auction. Salter was the last to carry the torch of what undeniably became one of Brooklyn's scariest haunted homes. It was torn down around a hundred years ago. Today all that remains are the legends of the ghosts of Melrose Hall. Travelers in the 1800s claimed to see the spirit of a young girl flitting about from room to room and looking tearfully out the windows. Others heard her cries as they passed by the mansion.

According to an article called "The Ghost Story of the Mansion in Melrose Park" in the June 22, 1884, *Brooklyn Daily Eagle*, Axtell had the house designed specifically to harbor war prisoners (along with his secret mistress) in its hidden chambers. "Until recent investigation divulged a secret staircase, opening into a closet on one side of the fireplace in the hall, the only mode of access to the haunted chamber was through the small stained glass window near the roof. In this room, the beautiful Isabella . . . is said to have perished from starvation."

Allegedly, Colonel Axtell had a mistress whom he asked to arrive at Melrose just before he and his wife and daughter came. The mistress was a "tall, dark woman of wondrous beauty" who set up her quarters in the secret attic above the ballroom. The only person besides the Colonel who was aware of her presence in the attic was his most faithful and trusted servant. She delivered the mistress's food every day without fail and accompanied the mistress whenever the Colonel called for her, which was usually at midnight and in the great hall.

The affair went on for some time in this way, until one day when Axtell learned he was to command an expedition on the frontier and would be away for an undetermined amount of time. He begged the mistress Isabella to leave, but she insisted on staying in her secret quarters and waiting for him, saying she would never leave him as long as she lived. Days went by, then months, then a year and Miranda, the loyal servant, continued delivering meals to the secret quarters until she became suddenly ill and died—before having a chance to pass her secret duties along to someone else. Isabella waited and waited for the servant to return with her only sustenance, but she eventually realized the woman was never coming back. She starved to death just days before Axtell finally returned home.

Melrose Hall was abuzz with celebratory preparations for the Colonel's return. Many friends had come by to welcome him home that fateful evening. He seemed happy to be back at Melrose, but he soon became curious about where his trusted servant was. When he was told that she had died, he was mortified, for her death would certainly mean the death of his mistress as well. The best account of what happened next was printed in the *Brooklyn Daily Eagle*:

> Suddenly the secret passage opened and the spectral form of Isabella entered. The face was ashen pale, each vein strongly defined on the emaciated features, her long black hair hung dropping over her shoulders . . . The apparition bore the look of unut-

HAUNTED NEW YORK CITY

terable sorrow, and the hands were clenched in an attitude of woe. Noiselessly, she glided through the hall—her sightless eyeballs bent on the petrified form of the colonel, while the lips moved in a ghastly smile as the bony hand pointed to the trembling wife. Nearing the entrance to the secret stairs, she turned and with her finger wrote the word "betrayer," then vanished.

This version has the Colonel killing himself on the spot, but a number of other sources state that he died in England of natural causes years later. The original story told in the *Eagle* differed on several different points from a story the same paper published eleven years later, on October 13, 1895, called "Tragic Fate of the Fair Alva." In this version, the dark-haired mistress was Axtell's sister-in-law, Alva (not Isabella), with whom the Colonel had fallen in love during his engagement to her sister, Margaret. Alva, the article said, came to the colonies on a ship from England disguised as a man. She then set up a comfortable space over the ballroom and never left the room for three years. According to that version, the Colonel was away for six weeks, rather than a year, but the servant he left in charge of feeding Alva died just a week after he left, and it was within the next five weeks that Alva suffered "the horrible torture of starvation without uttering a sound, for fear of exposing the man for whose sake she had sacrificed home and honor." All that remained was her skeletal body. A heartbroken and guilt-ridden Colonel Axtell then carried Alva's remains out to the yard precisely at midnight, which was their "special time," and buried her under an oak tree. He died three days later, after confessing to his forbidden affair. The day after Axtell's funeral, the haunting sounds of a woman's mournful cry and mysterious footsteps in the ballroom at Melrose Hall were heard for the first time.

The most recent mention I could find of the old Melrose Mansion, which was torn down in the early 1900s, was in the May 18, 1975, *New York Times*. An article, written by David Gordon, said that Melrose Hall's "dungeons" served as a jail for war prisoners. For many years following the Revolutionary War, it said, people heard Alva's "mournful wailing" and saw what they presumed to be her ghost drifting through the house. Before the mansion was leveled, "the bones of a woman who had been a patriot prisoner were discovered in the dungeon of Melrose Hall." Or was it the bones of the scorned mistress, Isabella? Upon his return home, and his grim discovery of the deaths of the servant and his mistress—both of whom had taken the secret of the tragic affair to the grave with them—had Colonel Axtell buried his mistress's skeletal remains in the dungeon to conceal his misdeed, rather than in the backyard as an earlier article suggested? It's likely that we'll never know. Every single source I found regarding the house and Colonel Axtell—and there were many—told a different story. So in this case, anyway, the best we can do is try to draw some sort of speculative conclusion from the many varied historical accounts.

A Miracle

In a country where more than 80 percent of people believe in a God who can perform miracles, it's not surprising that 74 percent of physicians—those who deal with life and death on a daily basis—believe miracles can and do occur. That's according to the Louis Finkelstein Institute on Religious and Social Studies of the Jewish Theological Seminary in New York City. The institute, along with HCD Research, questioned eleven hundred physicians in December 2004. Those surveyed were of varying religious affiliations—Jewish, Christian, Muslim, Buddhist, and Hindu to name a few—as well as atheists. Regardless of religious beliefs, an overwhelming majority of physicians—and indeed, Americans as a whole—believe in miracles, events we can't explain by known laws of nature, thereby prompting us to consider them to be supernatural occurrences or divine acts of God. New York City has certainly seen its share of miracles, often in the grimmest of times, for out of tragedies, stories of hope and survival usually spring. And although nobody knows who might be touched by a miracle, any of us—including our four-legged friends—could be potential recipients. The following story from Brooklyn made national news years ago.

According to a *Time* magazine article from April 27, 1931, a watchman at a Brooklyn coin laundry happened to voice his concerns to the engineer that the place was haunted, saying he had been hearing distant moaning that seemed to emanate from beneath the floors for quite some time. The engineer, problem-solver that he was, and not inclined to believe in ghosts, knew there had to be a solid, scientific explanation for the moans. Inspecting the floors, he came upon a sizable, boarded-up hole in the engine room where an attempt had been made months earlier to dig a well. Tapping a knife on the pipe in the hole, he was rewarded with the faint, sorrowful moans the watchman had spoken of. But the engineer knew at once that it wasn't a ghost. It was Bum, a puppy the engineer had found wandering around in January—fourteen weeks earlier. As he thought about it, he realized that the last day he had seen the pup was the very day the hole in the noisy engine room had been boarded up. The engineer pried the boards off the hole, climbed down into the confined space, and returned to the surface with a puppy so emaciated it was hardly recognizable; so weak it could barely stand.

The reason this story is in a book about ghosts and strange phenomena is not because the night watchman *thought* the place was haunted, but because it is particularly phenomenal that a puppy—or any creature—could survive in an empty well with no known source of sustenance or warmth in the middle of a North Country winter for more than three months. It didn't stand a ghost of a chance. But yet, somehow, Bum survived the ordeal. Some said the puppy must have survived on rats tunneling through the dirt; others called the whole story nonsense. I call it, simply, a miracle.

Coney Island Monster

The *New York Times* referred to it as "the Coney Island monster" on September 12, 1880, but nobody really knows to this day what the creature that flew over Coney Island more than a hundred years ago was. It wasn't a bird, for it had clearly distinguishable human features. It wasn't a plane, for planes had not yet been invented. It appeared to be a cryptozoological phenomenon known as a "flying humanoid."

Since the Victorian-era Brooklyn sightings, flying humanoids have been reported around the continent: in Houston, Texas, in 1953, when three people saw a winged man dressed in black land in a tree; in Falls City, Nebraska, in 1956, when a winged man with a demonic-looking expression was seen flying fifteen feet above the ground; and in 2004 in Guadalupe, Mexico, when a police officer saw a black, cloudlike mass descend from the sky and transform into a woman in black, who proceeded to fly straight toward his patrol car. The officer passed out, and when he came to, the flying woman was gone.

In the Brooklyn cases, W. H. Smith told the *New York Sun* in 1877 that what he saw was a "winged human form," and several other respectable citizens saw the same thing he had. More newsworthy yet was the sighting over Coney Island three years later. One witness, of many, said the creature was a "a man engaged in flying toward New Jersey," according to a September 12, 1880, *New York Times* article titled "An Aerial Mystery." The *Times* reporter gave the following description, based on interviews with many "reputable" citizens: "It was apparently a man with bat's wings and improved frog's legs. The face of the man could be distinctly seen, and it wore a cruel and determined expression. The movements made by the object closely resembled those of a frog in the act of swimming with his hind legs and flying with his front legs."

It was, according to those who saw it, deep black in color and flew at a height of a thousand feet. How this creature's menacing facial features could be seen at such a distance is not for this author to question; I'm merely stating the facts as documented more than a century ago.

Interestingly, the *Times* reporter didn't identify the creature as supernatural or alien or demonic, as we might have expected. Rather, the journalist seemed bent on identifying the "aerial apparition" as a "man fitted with practicable wings," saying that someone "has solved the problem of aerial navigation by inventing wings with which a man can sustain himself in the air and direct his flight to any desired point." He further stated, "Who is this adventurous flyer and what is his objective are questions of immediate and enormous importance." The reporter was certain the flying creature was a criminal taking advantage of his newfound ability to fly for his own twisted purposes, saying:

> Beyond any question, either the flying man or some scientific person at present unknown has invented the bat's wings and frog's legs with which the flying man now sails through the air. Why has not the inventor patented his invention and had himself duly written up by the press? The reason is obvious. The flying man is engaged in some undertaking which he cannot safely proclaim. In other words, he is an aerial criminal, a fact which explains the cruelty and determination visible on his countenance.

The article even offered the name of a possible culprit, a pretentious minister named Mr. Talmage, who, the reporter said, had "equipped himself with wings in order to study interesting types of immorality from the lofty height of a thousand feet . . . preparatory to preaching a scathing sermon on the wickedness and indecencies of our bathing resorts."

I'm not sure what's more bizarre about this story—the unidentified flying creature or the reporter's explanation.

The Haunted Brewery

The commercial property currently for rent at 315 Liberty Avenue *appears* harmless enough, if you were to drive by it today—and I'm sure it is, as no newsworthy tragedies have taken place there in a very long time, from what I could dig up. But in the mid-1800s, when it was the old Lanzer Brewery, before being sold to Piel Brothers, an unimaginable string of tragedies occurred there . . . and a ghost sighting to boot.

If you build a brewery, they will come. The early settlers of east New York were so confident that they could secure a good brewer to quench their thirst that they did just that. The original brewery that stood on the corner of Georgia and Liberty Avenues was built even before a brewer had been secured. Its first buyer was an Englishman who was a jeweler by trade, but that didn't stop him from making a fortune selling beer. He got out of the business while the getting was good. But the next buyer, Stien and Schillien, didn't fare as well as the jeweler and sold the old brewery to a German named Frank Lanzer.

The Lanzer Brewery's lager beer was immensely popular, and the business prospered under Frank Lanzer's capable management. Lanzer was well known not only as a successful brewer, but also as a Democratic leader in the mid-1800s. His influence with the Germans was so great that because he used an actual stick as a voting signal at town meetings, it became know as the "the rod that ruled that town." But along with his personal successes came a series of unfortunate events that seemed to curse everyone and everything associated with Lanzer. It began in 1856, when the original wood-frame brewery burned to the ground, forcing Lanzer to erect an imposing four-story brick, jail-like structure, and it ended when the Lanzer Brewery was sold to the Piel Brothers in 1883. By then the brewery was already believed to be haunted.

The first victim of misfortune at the site was Lanzer's old friend from Germany, who, according to newspaper articles of the time, went to the back of the building, shortly after the new brewery opened to a lot of hoopla, and cut his wrists. He was found the next morning in a pool of blood. Lanzer thought the incident would scare away business, but instead it drew in the curious and prompted unintentional advertising for the brewery. As business prospered, it became necessary to erect another two-story brick building at the corner of Liberty and Sheffield Avenues, which was connected to the brewery at Georgia and Liberty by a high fence. Some time later one of Lanzer's saloon keepers poisoned himself after finding out that the girl he left behind in the old country had married someone else. The next tragedy occurred in the "summer garden" between Lanzer's and a bar on the corner, where a man cut his own throat and bled to death after an argument with his wife.

In 1868, after thirteen years of bad luck, Frank Lanzer shot himself in the head at the brewery, and the Lanzer Brewery passed into the hands of his wife and sons, Frank Jr. and Charles. The bad luck continued. Mrs. Lanzer quickly remarried and became Mrs. Henry. Shortly after the remarriage, Frank Jr. fell through an open hatchway at the brewery and died instantly. Mrs. Lanzer's new husband took over operations of the brewery, failing miserably where Lanzer had succeeded. No sooner had management changed hands than another brewery employee shot his own head off after learning that his "pretty sister" had gone to a picnic the brother forbade her to go to. Finally, in 1874, the building on the corner of Georgia and Liberty Avenues, which was then reportedly owned and occupied by Charles Lanzer, caught fire and was completely gutted, with an estimated loss of $20,000. Between Mr. Henry's poor management of the brewery in general and the costly fire at one of the brewery's two structures, the Lanzer Brewery finally closed—taking its reign of bad luck with it. In 1883, the Piel Brothers purchased the block-wide property and opened up Piel's Beer in the old Lanzer Brewery. In 1895, they had the burnt-out structure on the corner of Liberty and Georgia torn down. The people of the neighborhood considered it haunted and unlucky because of its tainted past.

The October 9, 1895, *Brooklyn Eagle* said the old Lanzer Brewery was a place "that the superstitious people of the neighborhood have for some time called the haunted house. A few years ago, these people would go far out of their way to avoid passing it. This dread was occasioned by a story told by a young woman that on her way home late one night, she saw a headless man at one of the windows. Nobody else ever saw the headless man." But everyone knew it could have been any one of several people known to have died there. An earlier *Eagle* article from October 26, 1890, said the building was "known by old East New Yorkers as the haunted brewery. Not that many were ready to come forward and say that they had actually seen spooks."

Piel Bros. prospered through many decades of obstacles, including Prohibition, strikes, corporate beer producers, and buyouts. In 1959, Piel Bros. leveled the old Lanzer Brewery and erected in its place a new two-story building as their administrative offices. After Piel Bros. in Brooklyn closed in 1973, the building was again updated and remodeled, and it is now prime commercial space. For $35,000 a month, with an option to buy, you can stake your claim to a piece of history. And in this case, it was the ill-fated history of that street corner that makes it so shockingly fascinating, not the alleged headless ghost that made but one measly appearance more than a hundred years ago.

The Boschinsky Baby

Crowds of expectant people . . . lingered at dusk last evening, half curiously, about the ruins of the three-story brick tenement, 35 Moore Street, which has been demolished during the week. The building was torn down for no other reason than that it bore the stigma of a haunted house."

—*Brooklyn Eagle*, July 3, 1892

Nothing remains of the building that was torn down in 1892, right after a brutal double homicide that allegedly left it haunted and thus unmarketable. Today you see a nice, tree-lined street, a different building, and parking lots on the corner of Moore Street and Manhattan Avenue, where a little boy and his mother were murdered on December 15, 1891.

In the late 1800s, the Moore Street neighborhood of Brooklyn consisted primarily of Polish Hebrew and Russian immigrants. Frida and Max Boschinsky came to the country with their four-year-old son, Isaac, in July 1891. Six months later, Frida and Isaac were dead. They were found in their third-floor apartment at dusk on the Hebrew Sabbath Day with their skulls beaten in by a blunt object. At the time, for whatever reason, Max Boschinsky wasn't considered a suspect. In fact, several other suspicious people were arrested, but they were released when no evidence of their involvement in the crime could be found. It was an unsolved mystery.

The close-knit members of the community had their own theories, however, albeit unsubstantiated by facts. One rumor was that Frida had given Polish authorities information prior to her departure from Poland that ultimately led to some of her neighbors there being "flogged and banished to Siberia," according to the July 3, 1892, *Brooklyn Eagle*. The article, "Waiting to See a Ghost," went on to say that "the vengeful nihilities tracked her to this country and dealt out to her and her child the awful penalty of barbarians' assassination." Another, more probable, theory was that Max Boschinsky had fallen in love with another woman, Ida Bernstein, during the three years before his wife arrived unexpectedly to join him from Poland; and once his family arrived, they had to be eliminated so that he and his mistress could marry. It was no secret that the Boschinsky marriage was an unhappy one, mainly because of the husband's blatant infidelities.

Almost immediately following the double murder, the apartment building was believed to be haunted. Many men claimed that they had seen the pale, sad-eyed little face of Isaac in an upper window of the house. Some said the boy appeared "to beckon to them appealingly." The women and children who lived on the street were so certain of the claims that they covered their heads and looked down when walking past the house. Most people avoided walking by the house altogether, if at all possible. Because of the heinous crimes . . . or the ghost . . . or both, the shops on the first floor of the building closed shortly after the murders, and tenants began leaving.

One family maintained a tailoring business and took boarders on the second floor, but it didn't take long before "the boarders drifted away from them, one by one, and no new boarders took the vacant rooms." The tailoring business floundered and pulled out as well. According to the *Eagle*, this left the house, just six months after the murders, "entirely unoccupied, save by the alleged ghost of the murdered boy. Nobody in the neighborhood would live in the house [even if it were] rent free." The owner sold the building for $3,000 to a plate-glass importer named Wervoliski, and in July 1892, almost one year to the day that Boschinsky's family moved into the building, Wervoliski had the building torn down to make room for a two-story warehouse for his business. He was well aware of the popular belief that the building was haunted, and he hoped to quash the rumors once and for all by starting over with a brand new building on the site.

On the night of the demolition, so many people gathered at the site to see the ghost of the little boy that it required police crowd control. Everyone was certain the boy would make his farewell appearance, because it was, after all, the end of the Sabbath Day, and that was when the murder had occurred and when his spirit had always been seen before. But as the walls fell—walls that had trapped his troubled spirit in the house where he and his mother had died—he must have been set free, for he was never seen again—at least not at that place. But maybe the boy or his mother followed and haunted Max Boschinsky for the unsolved murder . . .

Almost two years after the house was torn down—two and a half years after the murder—Boschinsky was arrested. After coercing $100 from Ida Bernstein, to whom he was by then engaged, Boschinsky suddenly changed his mind about the marriage but refused to repay the sizeable sum of money back to the scorned woman. Bernstein went to the police, and in the course of questioning Boschinsky about his whereabouts and activities with her, officials grew suspicious of the many contradictory statements he made. Finally they concluded that they had enough evidence to arrest Boschinsky for butchering his wife and son. He must have been released, however, because the next—and final—mention of the man and the murder was in the *Brooklyn Eagle*'s September 14, 1895, issue, in an article called "Says He Is a Murderer." On that day, police discovered Boschinsky in the woods near a factory. His face and hands were bleeding from brush and branches, and they described him as ragged, exhausted, and guilt-ridden "as he gave himself up and called himself a murderer, saying he had been in hiding . . . and that his name was Boschinsky."

MANHATTAN'S ESTIMATED LAND VALUE IS CURRENTLY ABOUT $200 billion. But in 1626, it was sold to the Dutch West India Company for the equivalent of about $600 in today's currency by the Manahatta people, a band of Lenape Indians who were living in the area at the time. *Six hundred dollars!* Today, Manhattan is one of the world's leading cultural, financial, commercial, and educational centers. Though it may not be the most populated borough (it's actually ranked third with more than 1.5 million people), it is far and away the most *densely* populated, with a whopping sixty-seven thousand people living on every square mile. And it is the "host with the most" as far as New York City goes. It is home to the UN headquarters; Times Square, where a mystic named Kuda Bux once rode his bike in heavy traffic completely blindfolded; Broadway; the Empire State Building; New York University, which is reportedly haunted; the world-famous shopping avenues, Fifth and Madison; and Wall Street's financial district, which has made Manhattan the "economic engine" of the entire city. It was also home to the World Trade Center, now Ground Zero, until the terrorist attacks of September 11, 2001.

I could go on with all that Manhattan has to offer, but this is a book about ghost stories, and as luck would have it, many of Manhattan's most popular landmarks and tourist attractions are believed to be haunted. There's St. Paul's Chapel, St. Patrick's Old Cathedral, St. Mark's-in-the-Bowery, and the Trinity Church Cemetery; Central Park and its Wollman Rink, where two phantom figure skaters have wreaked their brand of mischief; the Ed Sullivan Theater; Merchant's House Museum; and John Lennon's former abode, the Dakota. Reportedly, the former home of Mark Twain at 14 West 10th Street harbors a number of ghosts, and the old Station House 2 at 84 West Third Street has a phantom firefighter who refuses to leave. There also are early reports of bizarre weather anomalies; then there's the interesting phenomenon dubbed "Manhattanhenge" which, although scientifically explainable, is still an awe-inspiring sight to behold.

Ball Lightning

During the storm of Friday . . . a shoemaker, living on the third floor of 611 East One Hundred and Forty-Eight Street, died of fright . . . He turned deathly pale, trembled, and crossed himself constantly. Just after a particularly startling flash, [he] walked to a window to open it, and fell back with a cry. He was picked up dead.
—New York Times, July 25, 1897

On July 23, 1897, a fierce and freak thunderstorm struck New York City and the surrounding area, causing a number of bizarre deaths, one miraculous cure, and many instances of a rare meteorological phenomenon called ball lightning. According to National Oceanic and Atmospheric Administration (NOAA) statistics, only about one percent of the population will ever see genuine ball lightning, and though it's been described consistently since ancient civilization, scientists still have "no accepted theory for what causes it," according to *Scientific American* online. But there are many scientific hypotheses that I won't even begin to get into here, since this is not a scientific book.

Ball lightning generally appears during thunderstorms immediately following a lightning flash. The luminous spheres can be the size of a pea or the size of a car, and they last from a few seconds to a few minutes before disappearing either silently or with a loud explosion. They can flit about like a spirit orb or zoom through walls and windows, and they can be orange or blue or white or yellow. They can cause great damage or none at all, searing a hole through glass or leaving no mark as they go though a wall or a human body. Do you see why it's so poorly understood? It's an enigma. The variables of ball lightning are so numerous that it's nearly impossible to categorize the phenomenon into any one neat and concise description. But whatever it is, it was plentiful on that summer day in New York City.

The July 25, 1897, *New York Times* reported on the "eccentric evolutions of lightning" that occurred that day, saying "fire balls" (ball lightning) could be seen "dancing among trees and about flag-poles and steeples." The paper also listed the many flagpoles that had been struck by regular lightning at the Manhattan Trust Build-ing, a Park Avenue apartment building, the Bank of Commerce Build-ing, City Hall, and a couple buildings across the way in Jersey City. The article, "Freaks of the Lightning," described a fireball the size of a baseball "that did curves and in shoots and other stunts that base-balls do among the trees" before vanishing. A woman on Vernon Avenue in Long Island City was horrified to see a fireball fly through the open window and knock a toy out of her baby's hands, rendering the child unconscious for a few seconds. The ball lightning bounced around the room before disappearing. Amazingly, no marks were left on the baby or any of the objects the fireball seemed to bounce off.

The storm's wrath was felt all across the New England and Mid-Atlantic states, including New York. Ball lightning was reported not only in New York City, but also in Poughkeepsie, where no less than three "balls of fire" tormented a single neighborhood, as if conspiring to do harm. But incidents of ball lightning weren't the only "freaks of the storm." One man was literally scared to death. The *Times* article cited earlier said that a man living at 611 East 148th Street "died of fright" after walking to the window in the heat of the storm. Witnesses said the agitated man turned pale, trem-bled, and "crossed himself" before falling backward with a whim-per, dead before he even hit the floor.

But sometimes a cloud can have a silver lining. One man on the Jersey side was blinded by lightning as he stood in the street direct-ing traffic at the height of the powerful storm. The lightning strike knocked him to the ground unconscious. His clothing was torn to shreds, his brass buttons were melted, and his billy club was shat-tered. But the man miraculously survived, and when he awoke, he found that the rheumatism and dyspepsia that had plagued him for so long were completely gone.

Stuyvesant's Folly

Housing near the exclusive Gramercy Park neighborhood is highly sought out by those who can afford it, and it's been that way ever since the first apartment house was built at 142 East 18th Street between Third Avenue and Irving Place in 1869. Rutherford Stuyvesant called the apartments simply Stuyvesant Apartments, but there were many naysayers who couldn't believe that well-to-do families would want to live in a "house" with other families. So the common name of the apartment complex became Stuyvesant's Folly, and the name stuck even after the tenement-living idea proved to be a huge success, especially among people in the arts, such as up-and-coming authors, actors, and artists. In fact, until the day in 1957 that Stuyvesant's Folly was torn down, it never had a single vacancy.

Stuyvesant's Folly was a five-story, twenty-apartment, red brick building designed by Richard Morris Hunt, who was inspired by the popular Parisian apartment building style called "French flats"—that is, luxury apartments. Over the years, many famous individuals lived at, or visited, Stuyvesant's Folly, including the widow of General George A. Custer, Henry Wadsworth Longfellow, Oliver Wendell Holmes, Edwin Booth, Central Park designer Calvert Vaux, Isadora Duncan, Queen Juliana of the Netherlands—and a ghost or two.

According to the September 22, 1957, *New York Times*, tenants at that time believed it was haunted by "soft-voiced, elegant women and somber, bearded gentlemen" who had lived there. But apparently the most memorable ghost was that of a French artist seen on the roof. There were originally four artist studios on the top floor. The Frenchman spelled out words of warning to those who ignored the arts. In 1957, the city's first apartment house was razed to make room for a larger, more profitable 249-apartment complex called Gramercy Green. The phantom French artist would be pleased to know that the arts are still alive and well in New York City.

The Ed Sullivan Theater

The Ed Sullivan Theater at Broadway and 53rd was built in 1927 by Oscar Hammerstein and was known as Hammerstein's Theater until its name was changed to the Manhattan in 1931. On opening night at the Manhattan, Gershwin, Sigmund Romberg, and Jerome Kern all performed their compositions, and Walter O'Keeffe was the master of ceremonies. The theater hosted numerous Broadway hits, including Kern's popular *Sweet Adeline*.

By the time the Beatles made their wildly famous American debut on *The Ed Sullivan Show* at the theater in 1964, it had become a production stage for TV shows. The Beatles were rocketing to superstardom, so their appearance on *The Ed Sullivan Show* jettisoned both the host of the show and the Beatles to stardom. It was a win-win deal, much to the chagrin of the stuffy musical program director who, at the time, said about the Beatles, "The only thing that's different is their hair . . . I give them one year."

After being called many things, including Hammerstein's Theater, the Billy Rose Theater, Radio Theater No. 3, the CBS Radio Playhouse, and CBS-TV Studio 50, CBS finally changed the official name to the Ed Sullivan Theater in 1967, commemorating the beloved entertainer's twenty memorable years in television. In 1974, Ed Sullivan died of cancer, but his legacy lives on . . . along with, perhaps, his essence.

The Ed Sullivan Theater has long been rumored to be haunted. Today *The Late Show with David Letterman* is filmed live from the theater-studio, and a team of paranormal investigators based in New York City actually participated in a skit on the show that aired on October 10, 2005, and investigated the studio after the taping. NYC Paranormal Investigations found video footage showing a dark shadow passing before the camera and an orb moving erratically, and they detected several unexplained sudden temperature drops and unusual electromagnetic field (EMF) readings.

Station House 2

Station House 2 of the Fire Patrol moved to a new building at 84 West Third Street in 1907. The Fire Patrol was established in 1839 to complement the work of the NYC Fire Department by salvaging and protecting the contents of burning buildings from water, smoke, or fire damage for insurance companies. Their job is not firefighting, but protecting property from the effects of a fire as well as water damage from firefighting. At the time of this writing, sadly, the patrol's three remaining firehouses were slated to be closed and the organization dissolved.

New York City was the first city in the country to form a fire patrol and the last to have one still in operation. Regardless of its history or necessity, the New York Board of Fire Underwriters who created the patrol would now save an estimated $8.5 million each year by letting it go, so Station House 2's days may be numbered, forcing the loyal firemen of 84 West Third Street to vacate the property. But that won't necessarily leave the old four-story building devoid of patrolmen. The good men of Station House 2 describe a ghost dressed in a firefighting uniform, 1930s-style, that occasionally appears and disappears before their eyes. They say he's a patrolman who hanged himself from a rafter after discovering his wife's affair. Though I was unable to corroborate that particular story, I found something else that might explain that ghost, as well as a lot of other interesting tidbits regarding the property, in the *New York Times* archives.

Prior to the four-story building currently standing at the Fire Patrol address, the location held a "disorderly resort," and on July 10, 1887, its proprietress was arrested for abducting and prostituting a fourteen-year-old girl and for keeping a house of ill repute. The building then became a boarding house, where on July 18 a year later, a cook named Alice Jackson was shot and killed by the drunken John Lewis. Lewis had brutalized Jackson, whom he had been seeing for a short time, so she had recently left him. The article said the infuriated man went to 84 West Third Street "and forced his way past the servant who answered his ring. He met the Jackson woman in the hall, and after a few angry words, shot her in the breast." The woman fought back fiercely and tried to grab the gun, but he shot her again, killing her. He was arrested and taken to The

Tombs—a gigantic jail on Centre Street in lower Manhattan now officially known as the Bernard B. Kerik Complex. A little more than a year later, Lewis was hanged for his crime in a quadruple execution along with four other "slayers of women" at the Tombs.

In 1939, in the building now standing at 84 West Third Street, forty-five-year-old fireman Alfred Stokes died of a heart attack inside Station House 2. The Fire Department's rescue personnel and physician attempted to revive him for half an hour with inhalators, according to a *Times* article dated August 11, 1939, but rescue attempts were futile. So if there is a 1930s firefighter hanging around the grounds in spirit form, as the current patrolmen believe, it is likely Mr. Stokes and not a mysterious patrolman who allegedly hanged himself there.

Manhattanhenge

Southern England has its mysterious Stonehenge, which is believed to be an ancient astronomical calendar, but did you know that New York City has a similar phenomenon dubbed "Manhattanhenge" by Neil deGrasse Tyson, the astrophysicist who documented it in 2002? It's one of Manhattan's most spectacular photo ops, with the sun setting on the center line of every cross street on the borough's street grid every year on or about May 28 and July 12, and likewise of the sun rising on the center line of every Manhattan street on or about December 5 and January 8. On those days, the sun can be seen in all its glorious brilliance setting or rising between the rows of skyscrapers on every straight street. This means that no matter which street you're standing on that runs east to west, you'll be witness to the phenomenon for a full fifteen minutes, weather permitting.

With Stonehenge, the sun rises precisely between megaliths that were somehow strategically placed upright in a circular formation nearly five thousand years ago, likely for the purpose of indicating the arrival of summer and winter, since the phenomenon in England corresponds with the equinoxes and solstices each year. Stonehenge is said to sit on a major *natural* grid point on our planet on a flat, barren plane, whereas Manhattanhenge was laid out on a major *man-made* street grid. Here, rather than the sun aligning between megaliths, it aligns between behemoth steel and concrete buildings erected on a densely populated urban landscape. And because the street grid was mapped out about 30 degrees east of geographic north, the days when the sun sets or rises dead center of every cross street do not correspond with the equinoxes and solstices.

In a city where everyone claims theirs is the "greatest show of the year," you don't have to pay a penny or wait in line to see the one that outshines them all—Manhattanhenge.

Merchant's House Museum

In 1835, when Seabury Tredwell purchased a three-year-old house now called the Merchant's House Museum, 29 East Fourth Street was part of the Bond Street area—an upscale, ultraelegant community of "Olde New York." The house was destined to become a museum from the start. The wealthy Tredwell family filled their classic Greek Revival rowhouse with the finest furnishings, and when Gertrude Tredwell, the youngest child of the family, died in 1933 in the same bed in which she was born, those fine furnishings—and more—remained with the estate. Vintage clothing, decorative objects, and furniture were all left in pristine condition.

Gertrude's sister, Julia, who lived with her in the family home, died in 1909, leaving Gertrude to remain there alone for twenty-four years, always obsessing over keeping the house the same in the rapidly changing world around her. Because of that determination, the home was already in near-museum quality the day she died. Fortunately, her distant cousin George Chapman acquired the home and its contents before it could be foreclosed on or, worse, demolished. It took Chapman three years to make the necessary repairs and modernization required to reopen it to the public, but in 1936, the house opened as the Merchant's House Museum, the city's only house whose interior and exterior have remained impeccably preserved for 175 years.

Today visitors are treated to a genuine taste of nineteenth-century upper-class life in New York City . . . but perhaps a little too genuine for some tastes because, according to the *New York Times* in 2006, the museum is Manhattan's "most haunted house," harboring spirits of the past. And the museum has a publication devoted entirely to its ghost tales called *Some Say They Never Left: Spirited Tales and Ghostly Legends of the Merchant's House Museum.*

Many people have reported seeing an apparition in the likeness of Gertrude wandering about the house. All her life, the woman staunchly refused to leave her family's beautiful home, even when houses on either side were being replaced by commercial property, including boardinghouses and tenement housing. So it's not hard to imagine that since her death, Gertrude's spirit has stubbornly refused to leave. Her house is all she ever knew, and it remains unchanged today, nearly seventy-five years after her death. Perhaps she returns once in a while to those familiar surroundings.

Vera Haller of *NY Newsday* online reports that a piano has been heard in the middle of the night and teacups mysteriously move from one room to another. Many people, including visitors and museum staff, have felt random cold spots, believed to indicate a spirit presence. In the 1950s, two caretakers who boarded at the house reported gentle tapping on the wall behind their headboards coming from a room adjacent to theirs. They were the only ones there at the time. Most believe that Gertrude is responsible for the ghostly antics, not only because she lived for ninety-three years in the house and died in the upstairs bedroom, alone and broke, but also because of a tragic love tale that made her a spinster. You see, Gertrude, the youngest of eight children, fell in love with a doctor, but the courtship had insurmountable obstacles. The doctor was Catholic, but the Tredwells were Episcopalian, so Gertrude's overbearing father forbade her to marry the only man she would ever love. Rather than venture back out into the world and risk having another relationship destroyed by her God-fearing father, Gertrude made the conscious decision to spare herself further heartbreak by remaining near reclusive in the family home for the rest of her life, if not longer.

The Old Merchant's House of New York maintains and operates the museum, which is now owned by the City of New York. The house-museum, a national historic landmark, is a member of the Historic House Trust and is listed on the National Register of Historic Places.

St. Mark's-in-the-Bowery

St. Mark's-in-the-Bowery at 10th Street and Second Avenue was built in 1799 on the site of the original Stuyvesant family chapel. Peter Stuyvesant, the Dutch director-general of New Netherland, was originally laid to rest in a vault under his chapel in 1672, but now his tomb is built into the side of St. Mark's Church—and some believe he's not really at rest, per se. The ghost of Stuyvesant has been seen, heard, or otherwise sensed practically since the day he died, making St. Mark's-in-the-Bowery one of New York's (if not the country's) most notorious and enduring haunted places.

In 1651, Stuyvesant bought a large tract of land in the East Village for farmland. "Father Wooden Leg," as the natives called him for his peg leg, used a walking stick and was said to be strict and boisterous, both alive, when it served the accomplished general well, and in spirit, where his forceful personality continues to have a big impact on those he encounters. When servants saw a ghost hobbling around the property just days after Stuyvesant's death, there was no mistaking who it was. And in 1774, when the Stuyvesant mansion was heavily damaged by fire, his ghost was seen once again, this time shuffling through the rubble. During the Civil War, a sexton of St. Mark's was stalked by a ghost with a cane and a wooden leg, who chased the screaming man off the property. But it wasn't the man's screams that woke the neighbors; it was the church bell incessantly ringing at the same time, even though nobody was inside the church to ring it. A few brave men ventured in to investigate, and they found that someone had torn the rope attached to the bell, though no person was found inside the church or seen fleeing from the site. The piece of rope still mounted to the ceiling was torn off too high up for them to reach, and the other half was found the next day—or so they say—right on Stuyvesant's grave. An article called "30 Years of Keeping Watch over Ghosts and Crypts at St. Mark's Church" in the November 17, 2004, *New York Sun* tells a similar tale, but set in the 1960s instead of during the Civil War.

There were many reports in the 1800s of people hearing Stuyvesant's unmistakable gait pacing up and down the aisles, but reports of his spirit haunting St. Mark's have dwindled considerably, though the legends live on—and certainly his legacy to present-day New York City lives on. And Stuyvesant's isn't the only spirit believed to haunt St. Mark's. A 1981 *New York Times* article claimed department store magnate A. T. Stewart and Washington Irving's "lost sweetheart" Matilda Hoffman also haunt the grounds.

Regardless of its status as one of New York City's most haunted sites, St. Mark's is dearly loved by the community. Throughout the twentieth century and into the twenty-first, massive volunteer efforts to maintain and restore the church for future generations have been undertaken. After a fire nearly gutted the church in 1978, the Citizens to Save St. Mark's raised funds to restore it, and eight years later, postfire reconstruction was complete. Since 1979, St. Mark's Historic Landmark Fund has provided for long-term care and preservation of the church and grounds—and maybe that's all the reassurance needed for Stuyvesant's ghost to finally rest in peace.

St. Patrick's Old Cathedral

St. Patrick's Old Cathedral at 260–264 Mulberry Street in Little Italy began construction in 1809 and was dedicated in 1815. In 1866, a fire gutted Old St. Patrick's, but it was quickly restored and remained the seat of the Roman Catholic Archdiocese of New York until 1879, when it became a parish church and the new St. Patrick's Cathedral at 50th Street and Fifth Avenue became the new seat. Joseph François Manguin, who designed New York's old City Hall, designed St. Patrick's Old Cathedral, with its intricate network of underground vaults and an eighteenth-century cemetery that surrounds the cathedral. New York's first bishops, including Bishop Hughes, also known as Dagger John, are interred there, along with founders of the Emigrant Savings Bank, a ratifier of the Constitution named Dominic Lynch, and the first American papal countess, Annie Leary. But Haitian revolutionary Pierre Toussaint, a current candidate for sainthood who helped raise money for construction of St. Patrick's Old Cathedral, is perhaps the most famous person buried in the churchyard cemetery . . . and the most publicized ghost believed to be haunting the grounds.

In 1981, the *New York Times* said that Toussaint was a "hairdresser and probably spy for George Washington" whose ghost now wanders around the grounds of the city's second-oldest Catholic site. Maybe that's because he's looking for his remains. When Cardinal John O'Connor began the cause-for-canonization process, he had Toussaint's body moved from St. Patrick's Old Cathedral to the crypt below the main altar at the new St. Patrick's Cathedral next to two other candidates for sainthood, Fulton Sheen and Terrance Cook.

Trinity Church Cemetery

Trinity Church Cemetery actually consists of three separate and distinct burial grounds in different parts of Manhattan: the Trinity Churchyard Cemetery at 74 Trinity Place, at Wall Street and Broadway, which opened in 1697; the Trinity Church Cemetery and Mausoleum, between Broadway and Riverside Drive, which opened in 1842 when the church ran out of burial space in its churchyard cemetery; and the churchyard at St. Paul's Chapel, which has its own haunted history and story later in the book.

The Trinity Church Cemetery and Mausoleum at the Church of the Intercession is where artist and naturalist John James Audubon's estate once was and where Audubon is now buried. According to a 1981 seasonal tour called The Ghosts of New York, apparitions of his likeness have been seen around Audubon's grave. Other potential ghost candidates buried at the cemetery include John Jacob Astor IV, who died when the *Titanic* sank; Eliza Jumel—a prostitute turned rich woman and the wife of Aaron Burr; Charles Dickens's son, Alfred Tennyson Dickens; and Clement Clarke Moore, who wrote the classic 1884 poem *A Visit from Saint Nicholas*, today known as *'Twas the Night before Christmas*. Standing in the peaceful urban oasis called Trinity Church Cemetery, one can almost hear Moore's voice whispering, "Not a creature was stirring . . ." and one can hope that it stays that way, at least among the tombstones.

New York University

When New York University (NYU) was first founded in 1831, the earliest classes were held in Clinton Hall near City Hall. By 1833, land on the east side of Washington Square had been purchased for the university, and the Old University Building was erected in Greenwich Village. But as the Washington Square campus became overcrowded, a much larger campus called University Heights was opened in the Bronx, and it became the base of NYU operations for quite some time. Then in the 1970s, the New York City government, including NYU, suffered financial hardship, resulting in the necessity to sell University Heights to prevent the university from going bankrupt. The Washington Square campus was spared, and after the merging of the University College with the Washington Square College, NYU began a period of revitalization and rising popularity. Today it is one of the premier research universities in the country. It was ranked as "America's #1 dream school" by the esteemed *Princeton Review*. NYU, the nation's largest private university, is one of the biggest landholders in New York City, with a sprawling campus that encompasses both Washington Square Park and Union Square Park in trendy Greenwich Village. It employs roughly sixteen thousand people and enrolls nearly fifty-one thousand students annually. But regardless of its current glory days, the campus grounds and surroundings once bore witness to some very dark times. If ever a place *should* be haunted, it's this one.

Washington Square Park is smack in the center of NYU's campus, making it the perfect location for graduation ceremonies each year. Seeing the park as it is today, with students and staff strolling about the grounds, it's difficult to fathom that tens of thousands of skeletons are buried underfoot. Most were victims of the deadly cholera epidemic of the 1800s, which resulted in the necessity of mass burials, but others were hanged there before being buried in what was, until 1819, New York City's central potter's field. No wonder the *New York Times* in 1981 said that Washington Square Park was inhabited by ghosts. But that's not the only place on campus with a tragic past. A tragedy of horrific proportions took place in NYU's Brown Building on March 25, 1911.

The Triangle Shirtwaist Factory fire claimed the lives of 146 employees, 90 percent of whom were young women between the ages of thirteen and twenty-three. The Brown Building, on the northwest corner of Washington Place and Green Street, was known as the Asch Building at the time of the tragedy. The building was designed to set an example of what good, "modern" fireproof construction should be when it was built in 1901. But on the day of the fire, it became a ten-story brick grave, as the exit doors had been bolted shut to prevent the workers from leaving early . . . and the only people with keys to open them, the management, took off at the first sign of smoke. The Shirtwaist Factory was located on the top three floors. When the fire broke out, it was fueled by scraps of flammable garment material strewn about the floor under the sewing tables of the workers. Within just fifteen minutes, fire had consumed all three floors.

When the hysterical workers realized the doors were still bolted, they headed for the fire escape, but it quickly collapsed from the weight of too many people, sending the employees hurtling to the ground a hundred feet below, piling up on each other. When the elevator stopped working, many others trying to climb down on the cables plunged to their death in the elevator shaft. Students from the NYU Law School, which was in an adjacent building, went to their rooftop and rigged two ladders together to span the distance between the buildings. Those workers lucky enough to make it to the rooftop could escape the burning building by crawling across the precarious ladders to safety, and many lives were saved this way, when all other options were failing miserably. The Fire Department had to move dozens of bodies of jumpers out of the way just to get their engines onto the scene, only to discover that their ladders were two floors too short to be of any use. Their safety nets failed, because they weren't designed to hold such a high number of people all jumping at the same time. Most of the frantic victims, in fact, were jumpers, but many others were burned beyond recognition or crushed in their futile attempt to escape the inferno.

Seven years after the tragedy, NYU leased and remodeled the ninth floor, where most of the victims had been trapped during the Shirtwaist Factory fire. The following year, the university leased the tenth floor, and finally in 1929, it acquired the entire building, renaming it the Frederick Brown Building. Today a memorial plaque marks the corner of the building at 23–29 Washington Place, where so many young women lost their lives. The Brown Building is not open to the general public but is used as NYU office space and for science classes. Students who have had classes in the building report sometimes feeling a sense of urgency to escape, or stuffiness, as if they need to get outdoors quickly to take a deep breath. But incredibly, that's all. There don't appear to be any spirits lingering from the Shirtwaist Factory fire; only occasional vague impressions of residual energy in the atmosphere that convey a muted sense of the desperate desire to escape that day. But other buildings on campus may be haunted.

The Old University Building was allegedly haunted by a young artist whose spirit could be heard pacing through the hallways. According to reference.com, the *San Francisco Chronicle* in 1880 said that the building had "an evil repute with the servant girls of the neighborhood . . . [who] have a notion that deep in sub cellars be corpses, skeletons, and other dreadful things." They were closer to the truth than we might like to think, because the potter's field in Washington Square Park was filled with just such "skeletons and other dreadful things." Then there's the NYU Library at Washington Square South, which is a stop on the Ghosts of Greenwich Village tour. The library is not nearly as old as many of the buildings on campus, but it has suffered a rash of recent tragedies, which always stir rumors of hauntings. In 2003 and 2004, several students committed suicide by jumping to a lower level of the library.

Brittany Residence Hall, at 55 East 10th Street, is probably one of NYU's best-known haunted buildings. It was built in 1929 as the Brittany Hotel, and it had a penthouse that doubled as a speakeasy during prohibition. Today the penthouse-speakeasy is a student lounge. Before it became an NYU dorm, guests at the Brittany Hotel included the Grateful Dead's Jerry Garcia and actor Al Pacino. Besides the intangible indications of the presence of spirit energy, such as feeling as if they were being watched or were not alone, residents have reported hearing unexplainable footsteps and music in the dorm.

And finally, there's the Third Avenue North Residence Hall, with doors that rattle and shake or mysteriously slam shut . . . all of which could be explained by wind or subways or any other plethora of atmospheric conditions in a megalopolis such as New York. But what of the doors that lock themselves? Or the objects that have been seen moving by themselves?

House of Terror

Even before Samuel Langhorne Clemens—pen name Mark Twain— bought the classic 1856 brownstone at 14 West Tenth Street in 1900, it was already supposedly haunted by former tenants. And even though Twain lived there for only a couple years and died in 1910 at his home in Connecticut seven years after moving out, his spirit is said to have joined the ranks of nearly two dozen others believed to have haunted the same brownstone at one time or another. In a 1974 book called *Sprindrift: Spray from a Psychic Sea*, Jan Bryant Bartell wrote about her unpleasant paranormal experiences while living at the townhouse for twelve years. The actress-turned-psychic-turned-author said that Clemens, author of *Tom Sawyer* and *Huckleberry*

Finn, was indeed among the spirits she believed haunted the building. She said Clemens appeared to a mother and daughter in the 1930s, twenty years after his death, in their living room. He told them his name was Clemens and that he was there on unfinished business. Sadly, Bartell's move from the house didn't end the hauntings that plagued her, and she came to believe she was being followed by the spirits. The troubled woman committed suicide in 1973, before *Spindrift* was even released.

But it wasn't just the widespread reports of the place being haunted or the book about it that earned the building the moniker "House of Terror." It was an unspeakable crime that occurred at that address two decades ago, which haunts us as much as any ghost ever could.

On November 2, 1987, a beautiful six-year-old girl named Elizabeth (Lisa) Steinberg was brutally beaten to death by her adoptive father, Joel Steinberg, who ironically was a criminal defense attorney. He was convicted of first-degree manslaughter. The crime outraged the nation and left the notorious address forever imprinted in New Yorkers' minds. And although little Lisa appears to be mercifully at peace, as nobody has reported sensing her presence in the building, her face all over the news in the days following the murder will never be forgotten.

For history or literary buffs not put off by its past, the townhouse, which is on a relatively quiet, tree-lined street in Greenwich Village, has a one-bed, one-bath apartment available as of this writing.

Central Park and Wollman Rink

In 1844, *Evening Post* editor William Cullen and landscape architect Andrew Jackson Downing persuaded New York City planners and commissioners to purchase and set aside a large parcel of land for use as a public park, before every inch of the city could be consumed by buildings and parking lots. In 1857, the city had purchased 843 acres of undeveloped land, including the old Croton Reservoir—today's Great Lawn—to create the first public park in America. The next year, Frederick Law Olmsted and Calvert Vaux submitted their winning design for the park, called the Greensward Plan. What you see today is their vision—Central Park. They could never have fathomed the twenty-five million visitors the park would eventually welcome each year, for there were only half a million people living in New York City the year the two gentlemen won the design contest for the park.

Today the park, which stretches from 59th to 110th Street, is always abuzz with activity, especially in the summer and fall months. But even in the winter, the thirty-three thousand square-foot Wollman Rink, which opened in 1950 at the south end of Central Park, draws an estimated four thousand skaters daily. There is an oft-repeated ghost story regarding Wollman Rink. The apparitions of two girls allegedly have been seen skating in figure eights over the years. At one time, as reported in S. E. Schlosser's 2005 book, *Spooky New York*, the apparitions were more clearly defined as two women—one in purple and one in red—who skated *through* skaters, then turned and looked back at them tauntingly and vanished in a fit of laughter.

A less familiar ghost story regarding Central Park occurred on a pre-1900 park landmark, which at that time was called Heiser's Hill. According to a *New York Times* article dated September 7, 1855, there was a "lonely stretch between Seventy-Second and Ninety-Seventh Streets" in Central Park West "near the centre of which is Heiser's Hill," and the ghost of "the eccentric German who gave the place its name" appeared there every night, precisely at midnight. But that was then.

Today, the ghosts of Central Park—save for the occasional skating specters seen at Wollman Rink—must stay predominantly out on the town, lurking in the historic old buildings on the outskirts of the park, such as the Café des Artistes.

St. Paul's Chapel

St. Paul's Chapel, a Georgian Classic Revival structure built in 1766, is New York City's oldest public building still in continual use. It was constructed in a field five blocks from today's bustling Wall Street in lower Manhattan, nestled between Vesey and Fulton Streets on Broadway, adjacent to Ground Zero. Not only did the country's first president worship at the Episcopal chapel, in the days when New York City was the nation's capital, but so did New York State's first governor, George Clinton. Kings, princes, presidents, lords, and famous celebrities have all knelt in the pews of the historic landmark, where at least one long-dead figure may still dwell. It is said that the decapitated ghost of Shakespearean actor George Frederick Cooke roams about the church cemetery searching for his head.

Cooke was a famous British actor of the stage and was hailed as the greatest early-nineteenth-century tragedian in England and the States. Ironically, the end of his life would read like one of the many tragic scripts he had performed on stage. Cooke made his American debut in 1810, but sadly, just two years later, alcoholism led to his death at age 56 in New York City. He had made arrangements before his death to give his head to science to pay for outstanding medical bills, and the decapitation was carried out as directed. But before being turned over to science, the skull was used in multiple performances of Edwin Booth's production of *Hamlet*. The headless body was buried in the graveyard behind St. Paul's Chapel, where a monument was erected in his memory by a fellow British actor in 1821 and still stands today.

According to Dennis William Hauck in *Haunted Places: The National Directory: Ghostly Abodes, Sacred Sites, UFO Landings and Other Supernatural Locations*, another famous ghost is said to haunt the church grounds: that of Civil War photographer Matthew Brady, who had daguerreian (an early photographic process) studios at 161 Fulton Street, as well as at 187, 205, and 207 Broadway—the last being just three doors down from St. Paul's Chapel. Although he became wealthy after producing a series of famous portraits of Abraham Lincoln and publishing a book called *The Gallery of Illustrious Americans* (1850), Brady lost his fortune during the Civil War, after outfitting twenty apprentice photographers to cover all bases of the conflict. He knew his collection would be historic and of immense importance to the country, but he misjudged the monetary gain its sale would provide. He died penniless in 1896, and Congress obtained the negatives and prints that remained of his Civil War collection. Only today are the value of those photographs and Brady's legacy in the fields of photography and photojournalism truly appreciated.

Hauck said an apparition fitting Brady's description has supposedly been seen on the sidewalk in front of the chapel, as if he's waiting for potential subjects to photograph. Several of Brady's studios were just down the street or around the corner, and Hauck said that Brady, in life, had spent much time approaching people who were dressed in their finest for dinner and a show, or proud

parents pushing baby carriages down Broadway . . . anyone who looked as if he or she might want a photograph taken. Perhaps he is still trying, in spirit, to earn back the fortune he lost in life.

More impressive than St. Paul's Chapel's age, historical significance, famous visitors, or alleged ghosts is the role it played in the aftermath of the 9/11 terrorist attacks. Although it is right next door to the World Trade Center site, the chapel and its grounds somehow remained unscathed by the collapse of the towers on September 11, 2001. That in itself is a miracle worthy of mention. Because of its location adjacent to the fallen towers, the chapel offered a refuge for rescuers and relief workers in the immediate vicinity, opening its doors for at least eight months to provide firefighters, police officers, construction workers, and searchers with a place to rest, eat a warm meal, and pray. Counselors, ministers, and even massage therapists were always available to those in need of comfort and relief. The wrought-iron fence surrounding the cemetery of the chapel was seen by millions the world over when, in the days following the tragedy, it became a "grieving wall," where thousands of wanted posters and photographs of the missing or deceased were posted, along with sympathy letters and notes, wreaths, flowers, and more, left behind by volunteers.

Today St. Paul's continues to hold its services and the occasional concert or lecture, and it still provides a safe refuge for the weary . . . apparently from both the past and the present.

Kuda Bux

In 1945, a man rode a bicycle through busy Times Square blindfolded and, amazingly, without incident. Seven years earlier, he performed an extraordinary feat of firewalking in front of Radio City Music Hall on the corner of West 50th Street and Sixth Avenue. That man was Kuda Bux. Bux was a Hindu mystic and magician who performed unexplainable, seemingly supernatural stunts around the world in the 1930s and 1940s. He was born in Akhur, Kashmir, in 1905 and began firewalking at annual religious ceremonies when he was just fourteen. By the time he came to the States to demonstrate his abilities to Americans, preaching that all humans have the capability of performing such feats, he was thirty years old and already a worldwide phenomenon . . . one that nobody has ever been able to discredit or even fully explain.

X-ray clairvoyance, as it's sometimes referred to, is the ability to see through solid objects and describe or read what is underneath. To Bux, X-ray vision and firewalking were simply matters of extreme mental concentration in which a particularly intense link between his mind and an object was established. Developing his own abilities had taken twenty years of near constant practice and a very strong faith, he said.

According to the August 7, 1935, issue of the British Broadcasting Corporation's periodical *The Listener*, Kuda Bux demonstrated his ability to see through objects for the London Council for Psychical Investigation. The investigators were permitted to blindfold the man in a manner they deemed absolutely impossible for him to see through. A lump of pliable dough was pressed over each eye, followed by pads of cotton wool, adhesive tape, and surgical gauze wrapped securely around the head several times. And if that weren't enough, they finally placed a black mask over their foolproof work of genius and secured it with thick tape. They left only the nostrils exposed. The investigators then chose several random books from their own inventory, opened them up to random pages, and had Bux read them. The subject did as told, reading each page as quickly as someone who was not blindfolded, thus proving the mystic's authenticity. It's interesting to note, too, that although Bux was able to read through solid objects, or ride completely blindfolded and unassisted through Times Square without incident, when he wasn't demonstrating his gifts, he actually required reading glasses. And it was a cruel twist of fate when, in his later years, glaucoma caused him to lose his eyesight altogether.

Bux's ability to do the "fire walk" was no less remarkable than his X-ray vision. Hindu mystics have been doing it for centuries, but the feat is still mind-boggling and not entirely explainable by the scientific community, much like other Hindu feats, such as snake charming, slowing one's heart rate and breathing to the point of suspended animation, climbing ladders of razor blades, levitation, and sword swallowing. On October 20, 1935, in a *New York Times* article called "Indian Magic Again Puzzles Scientists," reporter Clair Price said that, in regard to amazing feats of "Indian magic," "the explanation . . . lies somewhere in the vast and unexplored field of supernormal mental phenomena."

She was referring primarily to Bux's demonstrations in England that year, in which he traversed barefoot a nine-inch bed of hot embers that were said to be 800 degrees Fahrenheit on the surface and somehow remained completely unscathed. According to the article, doctors and researchers were on hand for the London demonstration. They bathed and dried Bux's feet prior to the fire walk to ensure that his feet were free of protective silicate or any other chemical capable of preventing burns. The temperature of Bux's feet before he stepped into the hot coals was two degrees below normal body temperature, and they were found to be soft and dry, with no sign of callus or skin conditions. He was very calm and appeared unconcerned about the incredible feat he was about to perform. Under the watchful eye of many, including the press, somebody threw a piece of paper into the coals, and it immediately went up in flames, which Bux fanned out before stepping into the twelve-foot-long trench of hot embers. He then proceeded to walk spryly across the entire length, turned and walked back the length of it, and then turned once again and repeated the entire process before finally stepping out of the bed of hot coals. In all, he took about sixteen actual steps on the embers. Even the men raking the embers had to move away every few seconds because they had become too hot for them to tolerate, let alone stand beside.

After Bux stepped out of the trench, his feet were immediately examined by London physicians, who found them unharmed and—amazingly—two-tenths of a degree cooler than before the fire walk. For good measure, a brave yet foolish English volunteer removed his own shoes and socks and attempted to do the fire walk. But after just two steps, he jumped out of the trench and fell to the ground in pain. His feet were so badly blistered that he required immediate medical care.

Bux performed the fire walk in New York City in 1938 to an incredulous audience in the parking lot of the Rockefeller Center across from Radio City Music Hall. *Time* magazine reported a week later, on August 15, that Bux had indeed walked on fire live on the "Believe It or Not" radio program hosted by Robert Ripley. The *Time* article, "Fire on Air," said Bux took "three long hoppity steps through one [ten-foot] pit," before hopping out and into another ten-foot pit. The pits had been fed five hundred pounds of charcoal eight hours earlier, and by the time Bux stepped into them, the glowing embers had reached a temperature of 1,220 degrees Fahrenheit. The article summed it up by saying, "Attending physicians examined the firewalker's feet, found only one small burn where a coal had stuck to his sole, (and) marveled."

Wherever Bux went around the world, he always permitted investigators and skeptics to cover his eyes however they wanted and have him read whatever they wanted him to read. He never charged a fee for his performances or sought publicity. All he asked was to be recognized as a common man who had developed uncommon abilities through determination and practice . . . latent and seemingly superhuman abilities that he insisted everyone was capable of harnessing.

Kuda Bux, the man who had impressed the world with his remarkable feats, died on February 5, 1981, after seventy-five amazing years of wowing the living. He had made it seem so simple. "Courage and faith, that's all it is," he often said. Courage, faith . . . and a dash of Indian magic.

The Dakota

The Dakota is an upscale apartment building on the northwest corner of 72nd and Central Park West that was built for high society in the 1880s. After all these years, it remains one of the oldest and most famous luxury apartments in the city. Most people know of the Dakota as the place where the legendary John Lennon, who lived there with his wife, Yoko Ono, and son Sean, was gunned down in the front entrance by a crazed fan on December 8, 1980. But the Dakota has been newsworthy from the day it was conceived.

Construction of the lavish structure began in 1880 and ended in 1884. At the time, the Upper West Side was sparsely populated, yet building such an elaborate and expensive tenement was a financial risk that owner Edward Clark, the Singer Sewing Machine Company mogul, was willing to take. In fact, Clark named his crown jewel the Dakota because, like the Dakota Territory in those days, the apartment building was built in a remote area away from the mainstream population. But instead of its isolated location scaring off potential renters, as many believed it would, the view of the splendid castlelike apartments towering over Central Park West in the 1880s attracted wealthy tenants like moths to an open flame. Even before the building had opened, all of the original sixty-five apartments were already rented.

In more recent times, the list of famous tenants—besides John Lennon and Yoko Ono—has included Judy Garland, Lauren Bacall, Gilda Radner, U2's Bono, Paul Simon, and Connie Chung and Maury Povich. Though the building has always been well known in celebrity circles, its name—and image—became known to the mainstream public after Roman Polanski's smash horror movie *Rosemary's Baby* was released. Polanski filmed the outdoor scenes in front of the Dakota, but contrary to popular belief, interior footage was filmed on a stage in Hollywood, because filming inside the building is strictly prohibited. The cult classic instantly altered the public perception of the Dakota. It had always been considered lavish and awe inspiring, but now it had become a backdrop to horror. When reports emerged of the ghost of a little girl at the Dakota, it seemed perfectly natural that such a historic old place would be haunted. The ghost, dressed in nineteenth-century clothing, reportedly said cheerfully, "Today is my birthday," to an employee. Ghosts are often believed to return on important occasions, such as birthdays, anniversaries, and dates of death.

A *Time* magazine article from 1979 said the Dakota had several alleged ghosts, which might explain why John and Yoko—known to be open minded regarding such things—held a séance in their apartment at the Dakota to contact deceased tenants. According to *Mersey Beat*'s Bill Harry, Lennon claimed to have seen the ghost of a woman crying as she walked down the hallway. Later, Lennon, the quintessential dreamer and peacemaker, was gunned down by a deranged fan as he entered the Dakota. The "John" sightings started almost immediately. Some people claimed to have seen his spirit at the building's entrance. In one case, a couple said he looked so real that they almost approached him. Others said they saw him inside the building. One source reported that Yoko saw him sitting at his piano in their apartment, as if to bring comfort to her.

You can take in the grandeur of the Dakota—and walk in the footsteps of the late, phenomenally great John Lennon—from directly across the street at Strawberry Fields, a garden memorial in Central Park dedicated to him.

IN 1683, QUEENS COUNTY BECAME ONE OF THE ORIGINAL TWELVE
counties of the state and was named after the Portuguese wife of
King Charles II of England, Queen Catherine of Braganza. In 1898,
the majority of the county became the borough of Queens when it
was consolidated into New York City. With 2.2 million people,
Queens is the second-most populated of the five boroughs, and its
population is so ethnically diverse that the county is considered to
be the most racially varied in the entire country, with immigrants
making up nearly half of its residents.

Tourists certainly have no problem traveling to Queens. New
York City's two major airports are located there: LaGuardia in Flushing and the John F. Kennedy International Airport in Jamaica Bay.
Its haunted landmarks include Fort Totten, John Bowne's House
(the oldest house in Queens), the historic Kingsland Homestead,
Flushing Town Hall, and Harry Houdini's grave in Machpelah
Cemetery. There have been some unusual sightings in Queens too,
like the "mysterious wild man of the sea," who was reportedly seen
at Rockaway Beach in the late 1800s but never captured or identified, and a knife-wielding ghost that terrorized residents near cemeteries in Maspeth and Middle Village during the mid-twentieth
century. But there are only a few vampires allegedly living in
Queens, according to the Vampire Research Center in Elmhurst.

All's not to be feared in Queens, though. Mother Mary apparently
has a soft spot in her heart for the borough and reportedly makes her

presence known—and shown in "miraculous photographs"—to those who believe at the Flushing Meadows-Corona Park, where the Our Lady of the Roses Shrine is located. And Saint Irene is known to have shed tears at the church of her name in Astoria, where her "weeping icon" and a piece of her real index finger are kept.

Bayside Apparitions

In 1968, Veronica Lueken, a housewife and mother of five from Bayside, was driving in her car, praying for the soul of the recently assassinated Robert Kennedy, when she suddenly smelled roses. At the same time, she saw an apparition of St. Theresa of Lisieux, who told the woman that she would be visited by the Holy Mother. Just as the saint had foretold, Lueken reported her first encounter with the Virgin Mary, known as a Marian apparition, two years later. She was told at that time that many more visions and sacred messages would follow, and they did—more than three hundred—starting at the old St. Robert Bellarmine Church in Bayside. According to Lueken, the Virgin Mary gave her messages of a prophetic and apocalyptic nature regarding the state of the world and humanity as a whole and said that a Marian shrine should be erected at the church. As word of the miraculous visitations spread and Lueken publicized the prophecies and messages she received, thousands of believers flocked to the St. Robert Bellarmine Church to witness Lueken in ecstasy or just to see the location of the Marian apparitions.

The Roman Catholic Diocese of Brooklyn, which includes Queens, meanwhile investigated the alleged phenomenon, and Bishop Francis Mugavero concluded that no credibility could be given to the claims of the Marian apparitions or any of the many other visitations Lueken reported, including visits from Jesus, seven saints, and two archangels. Had they seen the "miraculous photographs" that many people have taken at the behest of Lueken since then, they might have been willing to investigate further. But at the time, they were unyielding in their decision. Some of the messages Lueken relayed were at odds with, or not sanctioned by, the Catholic Church, such as proclaiming that it was evil to take Holy Communion by hand. On March 23, 1997, the *New York Times* reported that Frank DeRosa, spokesman for the Brooklyn Diocese, said that he had never heard of actual saints discussing the evils of television or rock and roll with genuine religious seers, as Lueken claimed they discussed with her. He also had never heard of such seers speaking directly to saints, but Lueken reported speaking to many saints, adding to the Church's skepticism regarding her claims. The Church's official opinion, however, didn't deter the faithful.

By December 1974, the crowds of believers and the just plain curious had grown so large that St. Robert Bellarmine Church was urged to fence off its property and prohibit further meetings on the church grounds, because the diocese was now frowning on the whole drama. So Lueken and her many followers instead chose to meet at a traffic mall across the street from the church and hear the holy messages as repeated by Lueken into a public-address system. The twice-weekly sessions were also sold to the public in cassette format. But the traffic island was only a temporary location until a Marian shrine could be erected a few months later at the Vatican Pavilion site of the 1964–1965 World's Fair in Flushing Meadows-Corona Park. The site had been considered sacred ever since it was blessed by Pope Paul VI when he visited New York City in 1965. And the permanent home for the Our Lady of the Roses Shrine, as it would be called, couldn't come quickly enough. On April 2, 1975, the *New York Times* reported, in an article called "Ban on Outdoor Prayer Sessions in Queens Is Sought," that Bayside residents were growing tired of the disruption the Lueken sessions were causing in their community, and they wanted police action to get them out of the traffic mall. But the police said the worshipers were protected under the First Amendment and therefore could not legally be evicted from the traffic island.

Though Lueken, who was dubbed "Veronica-of-the-Cross," died in 1995 at the age of seventy-two, her work on behalf of God has never been forgotten, nor the sacrifices she made while dutifully getting out the Virgin Mary's messages. Our Lady of the Roses, one organization of Lueken supporters, has grown to sixty thousand members worldwide. Today the Our Lady of the Roses Shrine is under the stewardship of St. Michael's World Apostolate and its lay Order of St. Michael—the celibate men who dedicate their lives to promoting the messages of Our Lady of the Roses and who guard and oversee the shrine that Lueken was instrumental in creating. Several hundred people still gather for holy hours and vigils. Even though it's been years since Lueken's last Marian visitation when she was alive, many people believe the Virgin Mary still watches over the site, along with Jesus and the saints. And there are photographs that some say prove it.

Lueken often told people they should take a lot of photographs at the shrine, because the Holy Mother told her many "miraculous photos" would be taken there to prove that the site was sacred. It certainly seems to be true. While sporadic cures are said to occur to visitors at the site, reports of miraculous photographs taken there are abundant. The St. Michael's World Apostolate website, swma.org, displays many examples, along with Lueken's own explanation for those taken while she was alive to interpret them. "Our Lady of the Sky," a photograph taken in 1978, shows a figure in the clouds that clearly resembles the Virgin Mary overlooking the Vatican pavilion. A Polaroid showing streaks of light that take the shape of St. Michael the Archangel raising his sword to a "#6," perhaps symbolizing the anti-Christ, which seems to be swinging its own sword in a symbolic battle between heaven and hell. Another photograph taken by a Brooklyn woman shows the Virgin Mary statue smiling tenderly, even though it doesn't in real life, and several witnesses claim they saw it occur. There's also a photograph showing white streaks coming down from the sky, looking much like the hand of God attempting to cradle the horizon of Queens.

What's most interesting about these photographs is their similarity to examples of paranormal photographs taken in haunted locations. In both cases, people examine the photographs for evidence of the existence of the spirit realm: an apparition, light anomalies, spirit mist . . .

St. Irene's Weeping Icon

At 36–07 Twenty-third Avenue in Astoria is a small, ornate church called St. Irene Chrysovalantou Greek Orthodox Cathedral, or St. Irene's for short. And in that church is a small, ornate icon of St. Irene from ninth-century Turkey, which is always adorned with jewels left by visitors and supplicants. It is said that the icon wept inexplicable tears in 1990, as if the patron saint of peace, as St. Irene is known, was crying about the imminent war. The icon is a twenty-by-thirty-inch, jewel-encrusted portrait painting of St. Irene that was painted on wood by a monk in Greece in 1919. St. Irene's church has housed the painting since 1972, when the church was founded. On October 17, 1990, the day before the Persian Gulf War began, congregants at John the Baptist Church in Chicago, where the painting was on loan, said they saw the portrait shed tears. Five days later, the icon was returned to its home in Astoria, where witnesses claimed it continued to shed tears for a full month, leading church leaders to believe that St. Irene was sending a plea for world peace on the eve of war. The head of the Greek Orthodox Metropolis Genuine Orthodox Christians of North and South America took the divine message so seriously that he sent telegrams to the UN Secretary General, President Bush, and Mikhail Gorbachev, urging them to avoid war. Since that time, thousands of worshipers visit St. Irene's weekly to see the legendary icon and to pray.

Almost immediately, thefts of the weeping icon began. The first incident was an armed robbery that occurred in 1991. In that case, the thieves returned the icon to the church five days later with the painting itself unscathed, but the jewel-bedecked frame missing. Realizing that others would probably attempt to steal the icon for its jewels, the church had an alarm system installed. It was during this time that a rift developed or deepened between the traditional Greek Orthodox Church and St. Irene's Church, which is a member of a dissident sect that left the traditional church in 1924. The traditional church's position regarding the weeping icon, as expressed through the Greek Orthodox Archdiocese of North and South America, was that they had doubts about any tears being shed and also believed that the first theft had possibly been a hoax. But police disagreed, and the faithful of St. Irene's were outraged by the statement. The bishop of St. Irene's said he would sue the archdiocese for defamation.

The plot thickened when, in 1994, the Cigna Insurance Company accused St. Irene's Church of fraud after it demanded compensation for the missing jewels under its insurance policy with Cigna. So, while St. Irene's was suing the Greek Orthodox Archdiocese for $30 million for libel, Cigna Insurance Company was suing St. Irene's Church for fraud. Then, in 1998, a thief struck again, climbing through a window he broke and leaving a blood trail straight to the icon, but the alarm went off and the burglar fled empty-handed. The libel suit was settled, and the insurance company's investigation was dropped. But then a priest of the church was defrocked after it came to light that he had worked in a foreign brothel. If, after all that, worshipers still weren't scared away, then the saint must really be working miracles at the church of her name.

In 1996, an authentic piece of St. Irene's index finger was put on display. It was purported to be "the hand of St. Irene" and the only known relic from her ninth-century remains. Once again, busloads of visitors came to the church the year "the hand" was acquired. Today that sacred relic is kept safely in a church vault, and the little church in Astoria has become the headquarters of the Genuine Orthodox Christians in the United States.

Fort Totten

In 1857, the U.S. government purchased the fort at Willets Point just north of Bayside from the Willet family, where construction would begin five years later on what would become Fort Totten, which played a major role in protecting the entrance to the East River between the Civil War and World War I. In 1898, it was renamed for Brevet Major General Joseph Totten, a man with a distinguished military career who fought and served as chief engineer in several wars, including the Civil War. Totten assisted in the building of at least three forts that secured San Francisco and New York before his death in 1864.

In 1941, the seaside military complex became the headquarters of the Eastern Defense Command's Anti-Aircraft Command, and a few years later, it became headquarters for the Air Transport Command's North Atlantic region. In 1954, the fort became the headquarters for more than half of the Nike missile sites in the nation. In 1967, after the air defense command moved out, the base's one hundred or so buildings were converted primarily to military housing, but unused buildings were leased to nonprofit and governmental agencies for administrative offices. Then in 1969, the 77th Regional Readiness Command of the U.S. Army Reserves, which currently has troops in Iraq and is one of the nation's largest reserve commands, moved in.

In 2004, the federal government transferred 49.5 of Fort Totten's 147 acres over to the City of New York Parks and Recreation Department, which officially opened Fort Totten Park the following year. The park includes eleven historic buildings within a landmark called the Fort Totten Historical District, plus a pre-Civil War battery and a

13-acre parade ground with soccer fields and plenty of room for concerts, performances, and sports. Fort Totten is also home to the Bayside Historical Society, in the 1887 Officers' Club building, and the
Northeastern Queens Nature and Historical Preserve Commission.
The Army Reserve and the EMS Academy (Battalion 53) Fire Department of the City of New York (FDNY) occupy more than half of the
fort's total acreage, including several hundred-year-old buildings—
and they're not the only ones occupying the buildings, according to
witnesses. There are numerous reports that at least a couple of the
buildings are also occupied by the dearly departed.

A fireman with Battalion 53 claims that nearly everybody who
works there hears voices in Building 305 when they are alone. Sometimes the voices are right beside them, and sometimes they are coming from behind the closed doors of bathrooms and classrooms for
the EMS training academy. But when the doors are opened, the
rooms are found vacant. Lights and bathroom fixtures turn themselves on, and television sets change channels on their own. Shadows are sometimes seen under doors, as if someone is walking by
on the other side of the door in an empty room. And an actual
apparition of a woman in white has been seen floating across the
grounds. The legend is that the wife of a general hanged herself
when she learned of her husband's affairs. The two-story, red-brick
office building known as Building 323 is currently boarded up, but
photographs and temperature readings taken by a team of paranormal investigators led the team to believe that 323 is haunted as well.

Mount Olivet Cemetery

On Thursday afternoon while some women and girls were picking
peas on the farm of Mr. W. H. Ring, close to Mount Olivet Cemetery,
on the Newtown Road, they heard cries of "O Ho!" Thinking that it
was some person in distress, they left the pea patches and ran to the
spot whence the sound came. When they arrived at the brink of the
little lake in Mount Olivet Cemetery, they distinctly heard the same
"O Ho" but failed to discover the author of the peculiar sound.
—*Brooklyn Eagle*, July 27, 1884

Mount Olivet Cemetery, at 65–40 Grand Avenue in the Queens
County town of Maspeth, was founded as an Episcopal cemetery in

1850. The following year, it opened to all faiths like the nearby Lutheran Cemetery at 6729 Metropolitan Avenue in Middle Village, which opened in 1852, five years after a law was passed that banned any more cemeteries from being opened in the mushrooming Manhattan district. At the time the following events took place, Lutheran Cemetery was considered the main feature of the town of Middle Village and quite possibly the most important Protestant cemetery in the New York metropolitan area.

The last week of July 1884 was a memorable one for the residents of Maspeth, Middle Village, and Fresh Pond. Dozens of people heard or saw what they believed was either an escaped lunatic from a local asylum or a raving ghost. Those who heard him said his only utterance was a hearty "O Ho," which was sometimes loud and sometimes fading. It was heard alternating between Mount Olivet and Lutheran Cemeteries, sometimes within a split second of each other. Those who saw him said he appeared to be a thin, six-foot-tall man who was naked and as white as a ghost or lightly wrapped in the sheerest white garments from head to toe, giving the impression of nudity. But what was most shocking was the large carving knife he carried. No wonder the villagers couldn't sleep well and were afraid to go outdoors. Even the gravedigger and stonecutter, who admitted to occasionally hearing cries of "O Ho!" while digging or placing stones, were frightened by whatever it was, and they'd seen and heard a lot in their line of work.

For several nights in a row, the town constable of Fresh Pond, Henry Bosch, gathered a posse of brave men armed with shotguns to track down the specter and put an end to the madness that had overtaken the wary townspeople, but to no avail. According to the July 27, 1884, *Brooklyn Eagle*, after listening to some of the witnesses' descriptions of their knife-toting culprit, the town constable (a farmer whose pea pickers refused to go back in the field) and about ten other men set out through the woods the first night "to catch the 'naked man.'" As they approached Mount Olivet Cemetery, "they heard the 'O Hos,' but they came from the direction of the Lutheran Cemetery, about a mile distant," through thick brush, stagnant bogs, and swamps. The men, having second thoughts about their pursuit, returned to the constable's house empty-handed to find a crowd of women and children hoping the mystery had been solved.

After a few drinks in the local barroom for courage, the men, now a posse of about fifty, set out once again to find what the women were insisting was a bona fide ghost traveling between Mount Olivet and Lutheran Cemeteries. This time, they followed the "O Hos" to the Mount Olivet Cemetery, but according to the *Eagle*, "as soon as his pursuers hear his voice in one cemetery, he is suddenly heard from in another." Thus, according to the *New York Times* on that same day, the men "went tramping through the mud for almost a mile, until they reached the Lutheran Cemetery, where the mysterious voice ceased and could not be made to speak no [sic] more," at one point sounding as if it literally sank into the soil at the fence line. The *Times* article went on to say that the men returned to the woods the very next night. "The gallant constable again headed a searching party and the voice led them on a similar chase and sent them home puzzled and frightened." But the sheriff of Fresh Pond insisted that the people were "needlessly excited" and were simply hunting down an armed, escaped lunatic—as if those words of comfort would make the locals rest easier!

Search parties continued for about a week, until their efforts were finally hindered by inclement weather. Apparently, the weather scared away the phantom they sought as well, because after July 2, no further mention was made of the matter in either newspaper.

The Wild Man of Queens

In 1885, the *Brooklyn Eagle* reported that Rockaway Beach was abuzz with news of a "mysterious wild man of the sea" whom a group of men claimed they saw or encountered. Witnesses said the wild man's body was covered with red hair "as long as a horse's mane," and he was dancing with reckless abandon on the beach until he spotted one of the men watching him. The creature had a "peculiar screech" as he dove into the ocean. Though area residents were on full alert and searching for the strange creature for many days afterward, it could not be found. Nobody had gotten close enough to say one way or the other exactly what the creature was. According to *The Eagle*: "There is a pretty good inclination to shoot the hairy being, as a means of ascertaining whether it is natural or supernatural, but no one will run the risk of being prosecuted if it should turn out that the wild man is only an insane creature."

Good thinking. It possibly could have been an asylum escapee, as there seem to have been many at the time, but how to explain a mere human—madman or not—with body hair half a foot long? Perhaps it was an escaped primate from a local zoo or a variation of the elusive Bigfoot. The Bigfoot reported in more recent years had not been identified as such back then, but it certainly sounds like a typical Bigfoot report. After all, it did share several common characteristics of Bigfoot sightings: the piercing screech, the elusive nature, and the long hair covering its body.

In fact, nearly a hundred years after the above incident, and on the other side of the globe, an anthropologist with the Peking Museum of Natural History set up several expeditions to find evidence of a very similar creature that a group of county officials in the Hubei Province nearly ran over as they were returning to a meeting late one night. According to a *New York Times* article from 1980, the men spotted a large creature with red hair lying in the middle of the road. While it presumably slept, the men—balancing on that fine line between courage and folly—crept within six feet of it and tossed a stone at its behind to see if it were alive. Indeed it was, and it rose up on its hind legs and, luckily for them, walked lazily into the night, upright like a man. Though investigators were unable to find or capture the creature, they did elicit sufficient evidence to prove that something unusual had been in the immediate vicinity.

Footprints up to sixteen inches in length were found, feces that were collected and analyzed proved not to be human or bear origin, and hair samples of "some sort of higher primate" were taken off tree bark. The witnesses all reported that the creature was more than six feet tall and had wavy red, waist-length hair and no discernible tail. It walked clumsily, which is not surprising, considering the monstrous footprints that revealed a flat-footed creature (no arch) with five toes, three of which were fused together.

It's unknown whether unusually large footprints were discovered in the sand at Rockaway Beach where the "wild man of the sea" was seen in the 1880s, or if he was considered to be taller than the average man, as is typical in most Bigfoot reports, but we can assume it was just as frightening, regardless of size, because the *Eagle* article reported, "Every man on the beach goes armed, and the women and children do not venture out alone, day or night."

Meanwhile, half a century later and forty-five minutes east and inland of Rockaway Beach, another similar being appeared mysteriously . . . and then disappeared just as mysteriously. The subtitle of the *New York Times* article on June 30, 1931, reads: "Hairy Creature about Four Feet Tall Frightens Woman and Breaks Up Ball Game." In Mineola, Long Island, a dozen armed police officers were dispatched to search the woods in Albertson Square "for an ape-like animal that has been terrorizing residents in that vicinity." The creature was seen by several groups of people over the span of ten days, yet no one was able to determine what it was. It didn't appear human, but neither did it appear entirely primate. It was something in between, with a "brown chest covered in hair." As in the Chinese incident, witnesses in Mineola threw bricks at their unusual discovery until it escaped into the woods, never to be seen again.

As frightening as these encounters obviously were, it's interesting to note that all three creatures described as "wild men" never once attempted to turn on the humans who pursued or provoked them. And we call *them* the wild ones?

The Bowne House

Against all odds, John Bowne returned from exile in Holland to his home in Queens, where he remained until he died. But some say that he is still doggedly clinging to the property, which is now the Bowne House Museum, long after his passing. Bowne immigrated to Boston in 1648 and married the affluent Hannah Feake in 1656. The two converted to Quakerism, which was then a repressed religion in most of New England, so they moved to Flushing, where they expected a bit more tolerance for their religious beliefs, since other Quakers had already settled in the area.

Bowne then built his house, now the oldest in Queens, in 1661. Because the Friends Meetinghouse for Quaker religious services in Flushing wouldn't be built until 1695, he allowed Quaker meetings in his own home . . . that is, until Dutch governor Peter Stuyvesant got wind of it and ordered Bowne arrested for "aiding and abetting" what he believed to be an objectionable minority religion. But Bowne was as uncompromising of his faith as Stuyvesant was intolerant of it, so he refused to pay the governor's fine.

Stuyvesant's men promptly showed up at the Bowne Homestead in September 1662, took the baby from Bowne's arms and handed it briskly to his ill wife, who was pregnant with their second child, and marched Bowne away. He was banished to Holland to await trial before the Dutch West India Company, but that wouldn't come for a year and a half, When he was finally brought before the judges in 1664, he invoked a declaration of religious freedom that had been written and signed by other settlers in 1645. The Flushing Remonstrance, as it was called, became a precursor to the American Bill of Rights, and it ultimately led to the birth of religious tolerance in America. Because of the Remonstrance, Bowne was set free and returned to his family and estate in Flushing, and Stuyvesant was ordered to stop harassing religious minorities in New Netherland. In this way, Bowne had been instrumental in the American struggle for religious freedom.

The Bowne House at 37–01 Bowne Street has rightfully become a New York City historical landmark that, since 1947, has been open to the public as a museum showcasing about five thousand objects that once belonged to the John Bowne family and his descendants. Bowne lived there until his death in 1695. His wife, Hannah, had passed away seventeen years earlier. His descendants, Bownes and Parsons, kept the house in the family for nine generations, until the Parsons sisters finally sold it to the Bowne House Historical Society. Today a twelfth-generation Bowne, Rosemary Vietor, is the president of the Bowne House Historical Society, doing her part in a sense, to continue keeping the home-museum in the family. The society owned and operated the house as a museum for sixty years, but it transferred ownership to the Parks Department in compliance with its Historic House Trust agreement. In 2000, the museum closed temporarily for a $2 million renovation project funded by private pledges raised by the museum, as well as money from New York City and New York State that became available once the Bowne House joined the Historic House Trust of New York.

Anyone would expect that the oldest house in Queens might harbor a ghost or two, and according to local newspapers, it does. The November 1, 2006, *Queens Gazette* reported that a ghost from the Colonial era has been seen and felt in the Bowne House, and the *Southeast Queens Press* stated in its Halloween 2002 issue that the spirit said to roam the halls is believed to be the unflinching master of the house, John Bowne.

Flushing Town Hall

The Flushing Town Hall, in downtown Flushing, was built in 1862 and served as an assembly point for Union recruits during the Civil War until 1865. Like most town halls, it was the hub of civic and community activity, functioning in that capacity for more than thirty years. In the late 1800s, an extension was added to the building so that it could also accommodate the Flushing Opera House and Theatre. Famous performers such as P. T. Barnum and Tom Thumb took to the stage there, and productions like *Uncle Tom's Cabin* were performed until 1898, when the town hall and opera house began to be converted into a municipal courthouse, which would open in 1902, followed by a jail in 1904. A town hall was no longer needed, because in 1898, Flushing ceased being a town, per se, when Queens County, where Flushing was located, officially became the borough of Queens. But the handsome, two-story Romanesque Revival building at the corner of Linden Place and Northern Boulevard would continue serving its community in one capacity or another for many years.

It remained the courthouse until the early 1960s, while at the same time continuing to host community events, housing a bank in the lobby, and serving as the headquarters for Flushing's Department of Sanitation. In the late 1960s, during a rare period of vacancy, the building was spared from being turned into a parking lot when the Landmarks Preservation Commission declared it to be an official landmark, stating that it was a historic, well-preserved building and capable of serving its community for many more years. In 1972 it was placed on the National Register of Historic Places, but by then, after several years of neglect, it had fallen into a state of disrepair. Then in 1976, an enterprising local resident stepped up to the plate and acquired a thirty-year lease from the city to restore the building and turn it into a dinner theater. During renovations, construction workers claimed to see the ghost of a Union soldier climbing up the stairs. Experts believe that periods of renovation and remodeling awaken the spirits that might linger about a place, especially those known to be haunted or that have an especially historic and colorful past. So it might not come as a surprise that construction crews were witness to a radio turning itself on all the way across a room where they were working, according to a 2006 *Queens Gazette* article, or that people heard unexplained music emanating from the old ballroom and insisted the place was haunted.

Half a million dollars and four years later, the restaurateur's venture failed, and the lease was then transferred to a businessman who used part of the building for his own insurance business while renting out the rest of the building as office space. When the businessman died in 1988, the city sought to break the thirty-year lease with the man's widow, out of concerns over the building's vacant and deteriorating condition. The city succeeded, and in 1990, the Flushing Council on Culture and the Arts was chosen to manage the building and grounds as a thriving community center for visual and performing arts. Today, thanks to a well-implemented, multimillion renovation that began in the nineties, the building houses a 340-seat concert hall and theater, galleries filled with the works of Queens-area artists, a visitor center with exhibits and a classroom, offices, and a large garden that can be used as an outdoor venue. The Flushing Town Hall has returned to its roots as a hub of activity and artistic expression in northern Queens.

Speaking of returning to one's roots, if you see a man climbing onto the stage wearing genuine nineteenth-century clothing, you might want to take a second look and make sure he's solid. Some say the impresario of the Flushing Opera House still lingers, along with the Civil War soldier.

Kingsland Homestead

The historic Kingsland Homestead in the Murray Hill district is an appropriate home for the Queens Historical Society. The Dutch-English Colonial structure was built around 1785 by a Quaker gentleman farmer named Charles Doughty, and it was named Kingsland after Doughty's son-in-law, sea captain Joseph King, bought the home in 1801. Today some of both the Doughty and King families' personal items, such as notebooks and diaries, are kept on display. The home was originally built on what would now be 40-25 155th Street, but it has been moved twice over the years: in 1923, when it was threatened by a proposed subway through the property, and again in 1968, after owner, a Mr. Murray who was a descendant of Joseph King, decided to raze it for construction of the Murray Hill Plaza at the corner of Northern Boulevard and 155th Street.

That's when the Kingsland Preservation Committee, a group of concerned citizens who wanted the historic home preserved, stepped in, got the house designated in 1965 as a landmark, and had it moved to its present location a few miles up the road. It now sits at 143-35 37th Avenue in Flushing in the two-acre Weeping Beech Park, where it shared the yard for many years with the nation's first weeping beech tree, brought over from Belgium and planted in 1847. The tree was one of two New York City "living landmarks" until it died in 1998. All of the nation's weeping beech trees are believed to be descended from that one tree, which stood there long before the homestead was ever moved to that location. Today all that remains of the fabled tree is a stump, with a few offspring around its final resting place. The homestead, uprooted and transplanted onto the property just like the old weeping beech tree, has likely found its final home. But there are rumors that deceased inhabitants of the old house may still be searching for theirs . . .

According to many sources, including the *Village Voice* and the *New York Post*, the homestead is haunted. In fact, the historical society hosts an annual Halloween event for children at which staff share the most famous ghost tales and mysteries ever reported at Kingsland Homestead. One such story took place in the late 1800s, when residents of the home were awakened two nights in a row, precisely at midnight, by someone demanding, "Let me in!" When they went to the front door, nobody was there, of course.

In the 1970s, the Queens Historical Society acquired the homestead and, along with the Kingsland Preservation Committee, opened it as a museum on March 24, 1973. Today the museum presents exhibits and walking tours of the homestead, sharing its history—and ghost stories seasonally—in a number of lectures and programs. It also serves as the main repository for information about the 300-year history of Queens.

Houdini's Grave

Harry Houdini was a legendary escape artist and the world's greatest magician in the early 1900s. He died under suspicious circumstances on Halloween day in 1926, and is buried at Machpelah Cemetery in Flushing. Though he crusaded against phony mediums and spirit rappers, he was a strong believer in the supernatural and in the afterlife, and he promised his wife, Bess, that he would contact her from the Great Beyond with a secret message known only to her, if it was truly possible. However, two years after his death, Bess inadvertently revealed to reporters what that secret message would be, rendering it impossible to know if the real Houdini was able to make contact during any of the many séances held for that purpose by Bess and others over the years.

It has long been believed that Houdini's gravesite is haunted, as well as the spot where his Hollywood home once stood, where some people claim to have seen his apparition. And a 1985 *New York Times* article titled "Is New York Too Scary Even for Its Ghosts?" lists the magician's home on West 113th Street as perhaps being haunted by a handcuff-rattling Houdini.

There are a number of reasons why Houdini might still be unable to rest in peace: his grave has been vandalized and the bust of his likeness stolen or destroyed numerous times; his death was ruled as natural, a result of appendicitis and peritonitis, yet he had received numerous death threats just before his death and had predicted he wouldn't be alive much longer; he died on Halloween day, which seems highly suspicious for a magician who believed in the supernatural, especially since he was a middle-aged man in excellent health otherwise; and to top it all off, his beloved Bess wasn't allowed to be buried next to him when she died, because she was a Catholic and the cemetery is only for Jewish interments. Would any of us be able to rest in peace in light of all of this, knowing that the circumstances surrounding our death were still uncertain?

The Associated Press reported on March 23, 2007, that Houdini's kin had requested an exhumation of the legend's remains to prove their suspicion that he was murdered by poisoning. After all, there were a lot of people—namely, the fraudulent spiritualists of the day—who wished Houdini would go away and stop cutting into their profits by exposing their deceptive practices, whereby they tricked people into believing they had made contact with deceased loved ones. The fact that Houdini was buried in the last casket in which he performed an escape stunt, because the casket had somehow been the only piece of Houdini's props left behind prior to his next scheduled show, only adds to the suspicion surrounding his untimely demise. According to a November 2, 1920, *New York Times* article titled "Houdini's Body Gets Here Today," it was reported that, "Houdini, a staunch believer in mental telepathy, placed much faith in coincidence. This was borne out in the fact that the coffin in which he wished to be buried was in Detroit when [and where] he died. When Houdini's show disbanded last week, all the stage equipment was shipped to New York, but by a queer trick of fate, or coincidence, this coffin was left behind . . . coming to light a few days after the other baggage had been shipped."

Not only did Houdini allegedly take his magic secrets to the grave with him, even keeping them from his wife and assistant, but he also took the true cause of his death with him. His remains are buried in the Weiss-Houdini plot at the entrance to Machpelah Cemetery at 8230 Cypress Hills Street. The cemetery is closed on Halloween because of repeated vandalism in the past, especially of the Houdini grave. But a ceremony by the Society of American Magicians is held at the gravesite every November 16, the anniversary of Houdini's death on the Jewish calendar, to celebrate the life of the great magician and escape artist.

The Elmhurst Vampire Research Center

There are still a number of people living in New York City who call themselves vampires. The vast majority live the lifestyle, but without the bloodlust. They don't drink real blood, but rather "Blood Baths," cocktails made from three parts red wine, one part black raspberry liqueur, and a hint of cranberry juice. And they come out to play at night in one of the several city clubs that cater to vampires. But they hold day jobs, have families, and fit in with society in every way. As you would expect, many vampires, or "vampyres," as they call themselves to distinguish themselves from the bloodsucking type, are drawn to all things dark—bats, black capes and

Gothic clothing, dangerous seduction, and even coffins. Some have their teeth permanently sanded into fangs or spend thousands of dollars getting a custom set of fangs fitted to their bite. Black contact lenses are a popular item among vampire lifestylists.

Then there are others who consider themselves "genuine vampires," and they can range from those who drink human blood offered from volunteer hosts to those who kill to get their fix—and everything in between. The Vampire Research Center in Elmhurst was founded in 1972 by the late parapsychologist and vampirologist Stephen Kaplan, with the objective of identifying what Kaplan considered to be genuine vampires, questioning them thoroughly, and documenting the findings. Kaplan, who died in 1995 from a heart attack at age fifty-four, also founded the Parapsychology Institute of America and was the author of several books, including *Vampires Are*. Since his death, his wife, Roxanne, has operated the Vampire Research Center. A vampire census that the center conducted in 1981 revealed twenty-one "genuine vampires," out of 480 questionnaires sent out. Two years later, the number had more than doubled, and at last count in 1997, a thousand vampires worldwide met the "genuine vampire" prerequisites. Sounds like they must be everywhere, right? But rest easy; they're not. In fact, at the time of the last census, there were only two vampires in Queens and just twenty-five "genuine" ones throughout all of New York City. The vast majority of Kaplan-style vampires live in California. So what exactly is a "genuine vampire"? Let me begin by telling you what one is *not*, according to Kaplan and other vampire experts.

Vampires are not shapeshifters that turn into bats at night, and they are not immortal, although many do seem to live unusually long, retaining their youthful looks much longer than non vampires. Their bite does not pass vampirism on to their victims—but I'd hate to think of the disease and infection their bites *could* pass on. For the most part, they are like normal people, except for the minor detail of a daily need to drink human blood, with the urgency of an alcoholic requiring a daily fix of alcohol. But unlike the more common vampire lifestylist, who drinks only the Blood Bath cocktail, these "genuine vampires" truly believe that they require real human blood to operate at maximum efficiency, and usually they get it at blood banks or by cutting a willing partner, according to Kaplan. Occasionally, they bite—or worse, kill—to drink. Kaplan said that "genuine vampires" require only a few ounces of human blood a day for their fix, but when they don't get their daily blood, they become anxious, pale, and bloodthirsty to the point of stalking potential victims, just like Hollywood-type vampires or those of literature. And speaking of vampires of literature, Ann Rice, legendary author of *The Vampire Chronicles*, owns a condominium in the West 50s in Manhattan, where she no doubt compares New York City's dark side to that of her home in the supremely supernatural New Orleans.

Staten Island

STATEN ISLAND IS THE LEAST POPULATED OF THE FIVE BOROUGHS, WITH only 465,000 people living there, earning it the moniker "the forgotten borough," but its ghost stories are anything but forgotten. The first permanent settlement on the island was established in 1661 near South Beach. In 1674, Captain Christopher Billopp arrived from England and was granted a large parcel of land on which to set up his homestead, the now very haunted Billopp (or Conference) House, where history was made on September 11, 1776—and where unknown horrors are believed to have taken place. The island is the site of the gigantic Fresh Kills Landfill, which prior to its closure in 2001, accepted garbage from all five boroughs. After the September 11th terrorist attacks, it was reopened to receive the ruins of the World Trade Center and serve as a makeshift crime lab while police continued searching for human remains in the rubble that was taken to the landfill. Bigfoot-like creatures have reportedly been seen in the vicinity of Fresh Kills. Todt Hill, into which the famous—and allegedly haunted—Vanderbilt Mausoleum is built, has the highest point in New York City at its summit. St. Augustine's Monastery was said to be haunted before it was razed, but there are plenty of haunted sites still standing that you can visit. Historic Richmond Town has a number of haunted buildings, as does Snug Harbor. Kreischer Mansion, the Alice Austen House, and the Garibaldi-Meucci Museum all have reported paranormal phenomena. But I saved the scariest story for last. It's the story of a woman who lived in a mansion near the Bayonne Bridge in Port Richmond, and she was allegedly murdered by a ghost in a creatively heinous manner. Just when you thought you've heard it all . . .

Historic Richmond Town

Historic Richmond Town is a living-history village, one of only three in New York State and the only such village in New York City. Visitors are treated to several dozen buildings and sites that have been restored to their original condition and appearance from the seventeenth to the twentieth centuries. Furnishings, decor, the grounds, and indeed, even the staff look precisely as they did in their heyday. Living history villages allow visitors to step back in time, being greeted by hosts dressed in period garb and strolling through homes and businesses that are being used today exactly as they were originally intended. Richmond Town was created in 1958, when the original structures were moved to 441 Clark Avenue on Staten Island in a joint effort by the Staten Island Historical Society and the city of New York to keep the hundred-acre village as true to its original form as possible. And the fact that some of the original inhabitants of the structures might have come along for the ride, making themselves known in ghostly ways, only adds to the authentic feel.

Since it was identified as a locale some believe to be genuinely haunted, Richmond Town has played host to countless paranormal investigations and even the *Scared!* television series, in which the crew experienced a lot of unexpected phenomena. The Parsonage, which houses the Parsonage Restaurant, has long been reported to host paranormal activity indicative of haunting. Originally, it was the home of the Dutch Reformed church minister, until it became a private residence in 1875. Lynda Lee Macken's *Haunted History of Staten Island* tells of phantom moans heard in the building, lights that seem to malfunction with no reasonable explanation, and orbs that have been seen flitting about the house after hours, one time causing such concern that an intruder with a flashlight was trespassing inside that the police were called to investigate. But, of course, nothing was found to explain the strange light that moved throughout the house that night.

The Guyon-Lake-Tysen House, circa 1740, is also thought to be haunted. The farmhouse, which was relocated from New Dorp, still has most of its original woodwork. And it may have retained a few original residents as well. Apparitions of children have been seen inside when the house was closed to the public and locked up. Guides and visitors have felt and seen things they can't explain, such as cupboard doors opening on their own, doors that stubbornly refuse to open when they were working fine just moments before, and the subtle sense people have of someone brushing against them or watching them when they're all alone. Staffers have reported hearing someone walking around upstairs when they know they are alone in the house and smelling ambiguous, unaccountable odors. Objects such as toys and bedspreads are often found moved or disturbed, and photographic anomalies are not uncommon.

The Stephens-Black House doesn't have as much activity as the Guyon-Lake-Tysen House, but it does have perplexing door knocking that qualifies it as possibly being haunted. And at the Reyeau-Van Pelt Family Cemetery, where the earliest occupants of the Voorleezer House were buried between 1780 and 1860, unidentifiable apparitions reportedly have been seen.

With more than two dozen early buildings grouped together in one splendid historic village, all decorated with genuine period furnishings and occupied by staff wearing original articles of clothing, is it any wonder that Historic Richmond Town is thought to be haunted? If ever a ghost could feel at home somewhere, it would be in a place where time has stood still, just as they left it up to three hundred years ago.

St. Augustine's Monastery

The old monastery that once stood on top of Grymes Hill is the stuff legends are made of. Because it was believed to be so haunted, and because it certainly looked the part, the monastery known as St. Augustine's, or the Augustinian Academy, was rife with unsubstantiated legends. The most popular seems to be the "mad monk" story. Sixty-some years ago, a monk went crazy and began butchering his fellow monks. He then dragged their bodies to the underground levels of the monastery, where he proceeded to mutilate and conceal the carcasses, until the day his dirty deeds were discovered. Then the murderous monk was locked away in the lowest level (of many) for the rest of his life, where his cries and incessant clawing at the walls went unheeded. Until the cavernous building was razed, his cries were said to echo throughout the corridors, chilling trespassers to the bone.

Another equally dramatic legend tells of the monastery catching fire one day when it was a Catholic school, with eighty-two children perishing after the basement stairs collapsed, trapping them all in the flames.

Either one of these sensational stories should have made the news, yet I found no archived media reports supporting such claims. So the terrified deathly screams, the hurried unexplainable footsteps, and the disembodied voices so often reported in the ruins of the monastery must have come from a source other than murdered monks or schoolchildren.

The Augustinian Academy, built in 1924, was the Grymes Hill boys' high school, and one of the finest secondary schools in New York City. The educators were priests and brothers of the Augustinian order, who offered an old-fashioned education of the highest caliber to the hundreds of Staten Island high school boys who passed through its doors between 1924 and 1969, when the school closed as a result of declining enrollment. In 1970, the Augustinians turned the sprawling academy building into a retreat house. It was then sold in 1985 to developers who left it abandoned during a tangle of financial and legal obstacles. The building fell into neglect and was soon damaged beyond repair by vandalism and the elements. In 1993, Wagner College purchased the hillside property and academy building at a foreclosure auction for $3.7 million, hoping to restore it for use as, perhaps, student housing. But the continued vandalism and a devastating fire in 2003 left the building too damaged and dangerous to leave standing as was. In March 2006, the Augustinian Academy was razed to make way for a new dormitory or academic building to be built on the Grymes Hill campus.

A time capsule from 1924 was discovered under a slab of granite beneath the old clock tower, and Wagner College plans to keep the spirit of the Augustinian Academy alive by commemorating it in a location on the former site of the academy. It's too soon to tell if the spirits believed to haunt the old academy by banging on doors, ringing the bell in the bell tower, and screaming into the night will remain connected to the property, haunting the new dorm, or if they finally moved on when the last of the walls came tumbling down.

The Alice Austen House

The Alice Austen House was originally a one-room farmhouse when it was built in 1690. In 1844, affluent businessman John Haggarty Austin purchased it and turned it into a sprawling Victorian cottage that his family called Clear Comfort. Austin's family included Alice Austen, his very enterprising young granddaughter, who became one of the nineteenth century's foremost photographers, and it's for her that the Alice Austen House museum is named.

Shortly after (some sources say before) Alice Cornell Austen gave birth to her daughter Alice in 1866, the father abandoned the mother and infant. So young Alice and her mother moved to Clear Comfort at 2 Hylen Boulevard to live with Alice's maternal grandparents, John and Elizabeth Austen. Alice's uncle, Oswald Miller, taught her the art of photography at age ten along with the photographic developing process. From that point on, Alice began prolifically taking and developing her own photographs in a unique photojournalistic manner that was well before its time. In all, she captured roughly eight thousand images in her lifetime on glass-plate negatives. Today only thirty-five hundred are known to still exist, and hundreds are displayed throughout Clear Comfort. Alice lived until 1945, when she was forced to move out because of financial problems and worsening arthritis that threatened her livelihood and her passion. Clear Comfort had become neglected and faced demolition, but a citizens group pulled together in the 1960s to save the historic home and its grounds. Through their determined efforts, the house became a New York City and national historic landmark, allowing it to tap into certain funds from the city's capital budget.

Today a citizens group, Friends of Alice Austen House, runs the restored house as a museum for the New York City Department of Parks and Recreation. The museum showcases Alice's accomplishments and reflects her way of life. The home decor is true to the Austen family's lifestyle of the late 1800s. One of the high points of a tour of the premises would surely be Alice's darkroom, which remains much as it was when she worked her magic there.

Alice died in her sleep in 1952 and was buried at the Moravian Cemetery. It's a well-known fact that Alice left her beloved Clear Comfort reluctantly and with a heavy heart, which are two good reasons to return, even if it is postmortem. Many believe the house is haunted not only by Alice's gentle spirit presence, but also by a great-grandmother named Elizabeth Austen, who nursed wounded British soldiers during the War of Independence when the house was still a one-room farmhouse. There was at least one redcoat she was unable to save, and his spirit is thought to still linger there. Legend also has it that a man hanged himself from a second-floor rafter after a young lady refused his advances. When shadows are seen and unexplained footsteps heard, they are most often attributed to that unfortunate soul.

Vanderbilt Mausoleum

The largest cemetery on Staten Island, dating back to 1740, is the 113-acre Moravian Cemetery at 2205 Richmond Road. Adjoining the cemetery at the rear of the property is the Vanderbilt family's own private cemetery with a striking mausoleum built into the side of Todt Hill. The elaborate mausoleum is a replica of a French Romanesque church, and it's said to be the largest private family tomb in the country, which is appropriate for a family of such distinction. In fact, when William Henry Vanderbilt, heir of Commodore Cornelius Vanderbilt, built the mausoleum in 1885, it was designed to hold 72 coffins in the vaults, as well as more under the floor. Regardless of its spaciousness, guidelines were strict as to who could be buried in the fabled tomb. William Henry limited admittance to male Vanderbilts, their wives, and their unmarried daughters only. Married daughters and their husbands and children who didn't share the Vanderbilt name could be buried on the grounds, but not in the mausoleum. The remains of the patriarch of the family and fortune, Commodore Cornelius Vanderbilt, were transplanted to the tomb upon its completion. Because of vandalism, the normal weathering of the mausoleum and grounds, and a couple unfortunate accidents that took place on the site, the Vanderbilt section of the cemetery, including the mausoleum, have been closed to the public since the 1970s.

Before it closed, the tomb was said to be haunted. There were many reports of photographic anomalies, such as people who were in a photograph when it was taken not appearing in the developed photograph, and conversely, unknown people who were definitely not in the viewfinder when the photographs were taken oddly appearing in them on the developed film. Interestingly, the Commodore always believed that portraits provided a bridge to communication with the dead, so he carried a tiny portrait of his deceased mother in his pocket at all times, according to Christine Wicker, author of *Lily Dale: The True Story of the Town That Talks to the Dead*. Could the Commodore be manipulating photographs taken at the Vanderbilt mausoleum from the other side? He certainly believed such things were possible. Wicker said that Vanderbilt was so trusting in the powers of clairvoyants and mediums that he may have based some of his business decisions on their advice. And we all know how that turned out: he became the richest man in America at one time through his hard work and sound business decisions in the shipping and railroad industries.

Cornelius Vanderbilt was born in 1794 and married his cousin, Sophia Johnson, when he was nineteen. They had thirteen children, including William Henry, who built the family mausoleum. Shortly before Sophia died, Cornelius met Tennessee Claflin, a scandalous though beautiful clairvoyant who offered the aging man "magnetic healing" and otherworldly insight. After his wife's passing, Cornelius asked the lovely Claflin, whom some say was the Commodore's mistress, to marry him. She declined, so the seventy-five-year-old Vanderbilt married another distant cousin, thirty-two-year-old Ms. Crawford from Alabama, in 1869. He died eight years later, leaving $95 million out of his $100 million fortune to his son William Henry, whom he believed was best suited to carry on the family fortune. The remaining $5 million of his estate was divided among his daughters, his wife, the Church of the Strangers, and Vanderbilt University. His other sons were disowned in the will, prompting one to commit suicide.

William Henry—as his father had predicted—managed the Vanderbilt family fortune well, and succeeded in doubling it. Yet when he hired the famous architect Richard Morris to design and build the mausoleum, he insisted it be kept large yet simple. He rejected the first design, according to William Augustus Croffut in *The Vanderbilts and the Story of Their Fortune*, saying, "We are plain, quiet, unostentatious people, and we don't want to be buried in anything so showy as that would be." Can you imagine that kind of humility? At the time of his death in 1885, before the mausoleum was even completed, William Henry Vanderbilt was the richest man in the United States.

The Vanderbilts' contribution to the Moravian Cemetery is not only their incredible family mausoleum, but also the twelve and a half acres of land Commodore Cornelius and William Henry donated to the cemetery, along with the cemetery superintendent's house. So, if they want to manipulate photographs from beyond the grave, who are we to argue?

Kreischer Mansion

In a deserted industrial neighborhood near the Fresh Kills dump sits what many say is the most beautiful house on Staten Island. Kreischer Mansion, a stately hilltop Victorian at 4500 Arthur Kill Road, was built by Balthasar Kreischer, a wealthy brick baron, in 1885. The mansion is one of two identical homes that Kreischer built for his two sons. Surprisingly, they weren't built of brick but of flammable wood. And that fact would prove fateful a few years later when one of the two mansions burned to the ground.

The fire allegedly claimed the life of one of Kreischer's sons and a daughter-in-law. Though the deaths were ruled accidental, it was a well-known fact in the community that the elder Kreischer had an irreconcilable dispute with the son who died in the fire, for whatever that's worth. Since the fire, the surviving house—still known as Kreischer Mansion—has been reportedly haunted by the spirits of the ill-fated couple. According to local historians and neighbors, doors slam, unexplained banging occurs, and apparitions have been seen.

Many people have captured what they believe to be spirit energy in photographs taken at the mansion, according to the owner in an interview by the *New York Daily News* on April 6, 2006. And photographs posted on the GhostStudy.com website depict what could be orbs (or maybe dust particles, as they were taken during renovation), along with possible apparitions in the windows and mirrors. Another oft-told legend regarding Kreischer Mansion is that a girl was pushed into a closet by unseen hands and could not escape until someone came and broke the door down, because it was hopelessly locked and nobody was able to otherwise budge it. One can almost imagine the Kreischer couple who perished in the twin mansion being shoved into a closet by a mysterious perpetrator, in a similar fashion, and having the door locked behind them—rendering them trapped and unable to flee the inferno. Of course, that's pure, unsubstantiated speculation. But Kreischerville, as the neigh-borhood is aptly called, with its storied past, has a way of conjur-ing up all kinds of tantalizing possibilities.

For all of its well-known ghost tales and rumors of its tainted past, nothing could be more bizarre—or disturbing—than an event that took place at Kreischer Mansion only recently. On April 5, 2006, FBI agents raided Kreischer Mansion, searching for human remains after being tipped off by one of five people involved in the brutal slaying of thirty-nine-year-old Robert McKelvey. Major news-papers reported that an associate of the Bonanno crime family apparently had fallen from grace with the family's "soldier," Gino Galestro, after a dispute over money the victim allegedly owed the loan shark. Galestro ordered the execution of McKelvey, because of the unpaid debt and because "he talked too much," presumably about the family's criminal activities, such as arson, racketeering, and federal loan-sharking. The tipster told officials that after Gale-stro ordered the hit, other associates of the crime family offered Joseph Young, a former marine who happened to be caretaker of Kreischer Mansion, $8,000 to lure McKelvey to the mansion and kill him. He said the murder took place in April 2005, when Young called McKelvey to the mansion and attempted to strangle and then stab him to death, before finally dragging the victim to an orna-mental pool near the house and drowning him. The murderer and three other associates dismembered the body and incinerated the remains in the mansion's furnace.

Even though the victim's sister alerted police that her brother was missing soon after his disappearance, by the time the tipster began cooperating with the FBI, the furnace that held the remains had been replaced as part of the home's renovation into a clubhouse. Never-theless, Galestro, Joseph Young, and the three other accomplices were charged with murder, as well as loan-sharking, robbery conspir-acy, assault, robbery, and arson. All were held without bail, pending trial, which has not, to my knowledge, occurred as of this writing.

One particularly interesting tidbit I came across for this story came from an online forum called "True Ghost Stories and Haunted Places." A post was submitted just three months after the murder (even before the FBI was aware of it) by a member who had visited the mansion the previous year—well before the heinous crime occurred. At that time, the mansion was being gutted and remodeled by the owner, Isaac Yomtovian, who has owned it since 2000. He bought it with the intent of converting the mansion into a clubhouse for senior citizens who would be living in upscale condominiums he planned to build on the property adjacent to the mansion. But the person who passed himself off as the owner to the forum member was not Yomtovian at all. It was the caretaker (and soon-to-be hired hit man), Joseph Young. What was particularly interesting, and ominous, was that the forum member's name sounded like something an actual hit man would go by; yet he was clearly clueless about the events that would soon transpire. This poor kid posting pictures on a ghost site of a man calling himself the "owner" had no idea he had actually been dealing with someone who would become a real-life hit man roughly nine months later. The poster said that when he met the alleged owner, he was told that, although the man didn't believe the place was haunted, the kids were welcome to return at night and take all the photographs they wanted to, since he usually stayed up all night anyway. Many photographs were then taken—some with unexplained images on them—but other than that, it was an uneventful visit to the storied mansion. The fact that those kids naively rubbed shoulders with a cold-blooded prospective killer that night is far more chilling to me than any paranormal activity they had hoped to witness.

Several of the photographs taken during their visit were posted on the internet, including four taken of mirrors inside Kreischer Mansion. One mirror captured the reflection of Joseph Young as he stood in the background watching the kids. The rest had anomalies that excited a few forum members; they commented on what they believed were phantom faces in the mirrors and windows, and several members mentioned how angry those faces looked. I wouldn't be surprised if any ghosts on the premises were angry—either from dying in a mysterious fire long ago, or because they knew the smooth-talking caretaker was up to no good.

After a stint as a restaurant, the property has been under renovation and is being developed as the Kreischerville Active Adult Community by the owner, who had been unaware of the killing that took place there. In a May 12, 2006, article from the *Staten Island Advance,* Yomtovian said that one of his contractor's employees had recommended the son of an employee to him, when he was searching for a caretaker for the property. The son was Joseph

Young, a former U.S. marine whom Yomtovian later learned had been dishonorably discharged. In exchange for providing site security, lawn care, and maintenance, Young was offered rent-free housing at Kreischer Mansion. But that didn't work out (maybe because he was allowing kids to come in at all hours of the night and take pictures!), so Yomtovian asked him to leave but allowed him to move into a different apartment he owned, since Young had nowhere else to go. Young was soon evicted for not paying rent, which is far better than the fate McKelvey suffered at Young's hands for not paying back a loan. The last time Yomtovian had heard anything about him was when the FBI investigators showed up at the mansion with a search warrant and discovered that the furnace had unfortunately been replaced.

Today the valuable property, if developed as planned with a hundred-unit upscale condominium, would fetch a price of about $20 million, even with its lurid past. As of May 2006, the owner was in what he hoped were the final stages of review of the project with the Buildings Department so that he could finally begin construction of the condominium.

Bigfoot on Staten Island

The *Bigfoot Casebook*, by Janet and Colin Bord, lists three Bigfoot sightings in or near historic Richmond Town. While it's not surprising that a village representing old-time Staten Island would be haunted, it is rather surprising that there would be Bigfoot sightings so close to the nation's biggest city. When we think of Bigfoot, many of us think of the Pacific Northwest, home to most sightings of a creature alternately called Sasquatch and Bigfoot. We think of elusive, hairy creatures hiding in the remote mountainous wilderness. But there also have been several sightings of the sweetheart of cryptozoology right in Staten Island as well as Queens—namely, one wave of sightings in the mid-1970s and the other around the year 2000. Tom Modern, a columnist for the *New York Press* magazine, searched for Staten Island's Bigfoot in 2002 and chronicled his incredible findings in a column called "Trashquatch: The Hunt for Staten Island's Bigfoot." Modern camped out in what he called "Sasquatch Country," which is the woods surrounding Richmond Town, the vicinity of the 1970s sightings.

In those sightings, witnesses described what looked like black bears but walked like humans, and in one case the creature actually roared at what it apparently considered to be intruders. Several years ago, a local resident told Modern that he too had seen "bears" walking upright like humans in the area, and another man found suspicious large footprints in the snow leading into the swamplands. Just over an hour north of New York City in the Hudson Valley, footprints believed to be from Sasquatch, because of their sixteen-inch barefoot human appearance, were found in April 2000. The walking stride was estimated to be forty inches. When I try to walk with a stride like that, I nearly do a split! It would take a very tall, upright creature to walk with that length of stride, and it would take a very large, powerful creature to cause the sounds of woodland destruction that Modern heard in his search for Bigfoot.

Modern, who camped out alone in Staten Island's Sasquatch territory, heard the sounds of a large stick pounding against a tree, a large tree being snapped in two, and something very large and fast tearing through the woods. He heard trees being torn down and found evidence of that action the next day, and he heard what he believed to be rocks being thrown and smashed as if during a childish fit of rage. Clearly, Bigfoot doesn't like our kind of company.

Garibaldi-Meucci Museum

Smack in the middle of Rosebank sits a house-turned-museum that was once home to two very important individuals: Guiseppe Garibaldi and Antonio Meucci. Though the two died many years ago, their legacy—and perhaps their very essence—lives on in the Garibaldi-Meucci Museum. The house was built in 1840, but Meucci, the *real* first inventor of the telephone, and his wife, Ester, didn't move in as tenants until 1850. That same year, their good friend Garibaldi was in exile from Italy and came to New York City seeking refuge. The Meuccis insisted he move in with them, so he stayed on for four years, working with Meucci in his candle factory. In 1854, Garibaldi returned to Italy, where he became an Italian revolutionary war hero for leading the victories that unified Italy. Thirty years later, upon his death, a marble plaque commemorating his heroism was placed over the front door of the house he shared with Meucci.

Though Garibaldi died a hero, his friend Meucci, whose contribution to society was also monumental, died wrongfully impoverished. But on June 16, 2002, the House of Representatives recognized Meucci as the actual inventor of the first telephone, rather than Alexander Graham Bell. Meucci had discovered that sounds travel through copper wires by electrical impulses while working with patients using therapeutic electrical shock. The brilliant inventor then used this knowledge several years later to create a device to communicate with his bedridden and paralyzed wife while he was in his workshop. In 1860, he demonstrated his "talking telegraph," or "teletrefono," as he called it, in New York City, but he didn't have the $250 to pay for the patent. Meanwhile, Alexander Graham Bell was sharing a lab with Meucci, and he *did* have enough money for a patent on the device. He allegedly tweaked Meucci's prototype design, to which he had access in their shared lab, and submitted it for a patent in his own name in 1876. Bell went on to enjoy the fame and fortune from inventing the first telephone, while Meucci struggled just to stay out of poverty. In 1899, the Supreme Court agreed to hear the case of fraud against Bell, but Meucci died that year, so the charges were dropped. Finally, in 2002, Meucci got the recognition he deserved posthumously, but even though his spirit may no longer have that "unfinished business" keeping him from crossing over, apparently someone else's spirit has reason to linger, as the museum is said to be haunted.

Garibaldi died in 1884 and Meucci in 1899. After Meucci's death, the Italian community acquired the house to preserve as a memorial to their war hero. In 1907, the house was moved to its current location at the corner of Tompkins and Chestnut Avenues, and in 1919, it was turned over to the Order Sons of Italy in America, who continue to own and operate it today. The house was restored and filled with Italian artifacts before opening as the Garibaldi-Meucci Museum in 1956. The museum offers historical, educational, and now paranormal programs, including Ghost Hunter's University, sponsored by *Haunted Times* magazine. The unique training takes place only at recognized haunted locations, so the museum joins such paranormal hotspots as Eastern State Penitentiary and the Lizzie Borden Bed and Breakfast. The museum's newest program is called Haunted Tour at the Garibaldi-Meucci Museum, where participants learn about the history and the people associated with the museum for the last 160 years, along with speculation about who may be haunting the museum.

The staffers have enough of their own strange experiences to warrant the haunted tour they now offer, and paranormal investigators have enjoyed success in obtaining evidence suggesting a genuine haunting. According to the museum's official website, the Staten Island Paranormal Society has captured evidence of spirit energy, such as orbs, in digital photographs and spirit conversations (EVPs) on digital voice recorders.

Snug Harbor

Sailors Snug Harbor was a 140-acre property along the Kill van Kull Waterway that was developed in 1833 as a home and hospital for retired seamen. It was the first such facility in the United States. Even though it was the brainchild of Robert Randall, the son of a wealthy sea merchant, the institution never came to fruition until thirty-some years after Randall's death. But in his will, Randall left the majority of his inherited fortune to fully fund the construction of a marine hospital that would maintain and support "aged, decrepit, and worn-out sailors" from all nations, be they naval seamen or merchant marines. The only requisite was that old sailors had to attend regular prayer services, say grace before meals, stay sober, and be in bed by 9 P.M. In short, they had to convert to gentlemanly behavior, but it was worth it to many who had lived rough, unstructured lives on the seas. At Snug Harbor, they always had a warm bed and warm food, as well as the familiar smells and sounds of the sea to which they were so accustomed.

Snug Harbor was home to a thousand seamen in 1900—in the days before other retirement options—but by the mid-fifties, occupancy had dropped to one-fifth of that. Several buildings had to be demolished to reduce the cost of maintaining unnecessary buildings for its dwindling population. After running the risk of being razed in the 1960s, six of the remaining buildings were designated as landmarks by the New York City Landmarks Preservation Commission. That designation ultimately led to the site's purchase by the City of New York, which took possession of the property in 1976 after removing the 110 sailors still enrolled on the grounds to new quarters in Sea Level, North Carolina. That same year, the old

Sailors Snug Harbor became the new eighty-three-acre Snug Harbor Cultural Center, which today boasts a botanical garden, children's museum, maritime collection, music hall, classrooms, offices, and the Art Lab Art School. Snug Harbor has become "one of the largest adaptive reuse sites in the country," according to its website. The many renovated buildings and their specific purposes are as diverse as the ghosts that appear to haunt them. In fact, the Snug Harbor Cultural Center is so haunted that it even occasionally hosts guided ghost tours on the grounds.

The Governor's House and Victorian Cottages, where resident artists from around the world can set up their studios, are thought to be especially haunted. According to author Lynda Lee Macken, there have been sightings of a weeping lady dressed in white who vanishes into thin air near Cottage 3. Ghostly presences are felt so often by park staff that they've even named some of the more prolific spectral visitors: the Older Matron, Old Salt, and the Music Hall Ghost, according to Macken. The third ghost has been seen in the balcony of the music hall.

In the Matron's House, people have reported mysterious noises, and seeing apparitions of a lady looking out the second-floor window of the bedroom in which a stillborn, illegitimate child was born to a young woman who never recovered from the shock of her loss.

Richard Randall also has every reason to haunt the grounds he envisioned and financed . . . yet never saw become a reality in his lifetime. Not only was his grave moved from its original resting place at Trinity Church Cemetery in Manhattan to Sailors Snug Harbor, but a bronze statue in his likeness that was erected in 1878 was also moved a hundred years later, when the city of New York took ownership of Snug Harbor and sent the statue packing along with the remaining residents to Sea Level, North Carolina. Though Randall's remains and the statue have "moved on," the spirit essence of Randall may still remain.

The Conference House

The Conference House, also known as the Billopp House, was originally called the Manor of Bentley. It overlooks Raritan Bay on the southernmost tip of Staten Island in the Tottenville area. Built around 1680, the house derives its names from a historic event that took place there in 1776, and from two of its illustrious owners, Captain Christopher Billopp, who built the house, and his great-grandson Colonel Christopher Billopp.

It seems that the Billopp men may have left behind more than the house and its legacy when they died. Because of their actions, it's believed that several spirits dwell in the remarkably haunted Conference House. In a house with such a long history of reported paranormal activity by such a vast number of people, including visitors, staff, and caretakers, it would be a mistake to discount the possibility that the Conference House is genuinely haunted. And as is often the case in historical hauntings, the history itself is every bit as riveting.

Captain Christopher Billopp served England well when he sailed to America in 1674. So well, in fact, that his good work was recognized by the governor of the New York colony. Thomas Dongan granted Billopp, as his just reward, sixteen hundred acres of prime Staten Island land at the southernmost tip of New York, where Billopp built an imposing stone house around 1680. Though modest by today's standards, the two-story house, which still stands, was considered superior for its day. It consisted of a basement with kitchen, two floors of living quarters, and a dimly lit, stuffy attic with plenty of room for a number of servants to sleep.

After serving the British Navy, Captain Billopp continued to prosper, operating a ferry service in the area. He seemed to live a charmed life, yet despite his outstanding service to his country, the grandeur of the land and manor he owned, and his Midas-touch business ventures, Captain Billopp, the man, had questionable virtue within his own household. With his slaves and acquaintances, he was unforgiving and ruthless, and according to Lynda Lee Macken in *Haunted History of Staten Island*, the captain was charged with assault at least twice, once in the colonies and then later in England. Several sources say he killed a young female slave on the stairway landing in the Conference House with a fireplace poker when she rejected his advances, and a psychic sensed a similar scenario without prior knowledge of the rumor.

The Captain's great-grandson, Colonel Christopher Billopp, was known to be just as violent and cruel. But what he's most remembered for is the historic three-hour peace conference held on September 11, 1776, at his very residence—hence, the name Conference House. The conference was arranged by the king of England in an effort to thwart the likelihood of an all-out war for independence between England and the colonies, which had just penned the Declaration of Independence. It was hosted by Colonel Billopp; after all, his was the grandest house on the island at the time, and the Billopp family was well acquainted with British royalty. The king dispatched Lord Admiral Richard Howe to speak on his behalf, warning Howe that under no circumstances would the colonies be granted independence. In other words, this wasn't truly a negotiation at all, but a meeting to relay a message. Attending on behalf of the colonies were Benjamin Franklin, John Adams, and Edward Rutledge, and they had no illusions that England would bow to their demands, but Franklin was curious as to what the king had to say. When it became obvious that neither side was going to give even an inch, Franklin and his comrades quickly left. So much for the peace conference. War was inevitable. And that's when things really got interesting at the old Billopp House.

Colonel Billopp, because of his well-known loyalty to the British throne, was kidnapped and subsequently imprisoned several times by the Americans. The suspicious man came to believe that someone living in his house must be betraying him. One day he allegedly saw a young servant girl place a lantern in an upstairs bedroom window facing St. Peter's Church in Perth Amboy, across Raritan Bay. Believing she was the one who had been signaling Colonial troops that he was home, he chased the horrified girl to the stairs, where she either stumbled and fell or was shoved all the way down the stairs, breaking her neck. The state of New York soon confiscated all property belonging to pro-British colonists, so Billopp was forced to flee the country and move to Nova Scotia, where the king of England gifted him with land. After nearly a hundred years in the Billopp family, the Conference House began a period of private ownership that lasted until the 1920s.

A huge amount of paranormal phenomena has been reported by people who have lived at, worked at, visited, or investigated the Conference House. Inexplicable shadows have been seen over the years, as well as apparitions of a young lady on the stair landing. Objects, especially old portraits and candles, are found moved from their original location. Candles get mysteriously snuffed out. Unexplained sounds, such as soldiers' drums beating and a woman singing mournfully, have been heard on more than one occasion. A woman's terrified screams have also been heard, and several people have been tapped or had their hair tousled by something unseen. At least one British soldier has been sighted, as well as a woman looking out the second-floor window. There seems to be no doubt that the house is haunted. The question, then, is why and by whom? Is it the young slave who spurned the Captain's advances or otherwise provoked him to the point of murder? Or could it be the ghost of the servant that the Colonel believed betrayed him? Is the house being haunted by the British soldiers believed to have been buried on the grounds at a time when the basement kitchen was purportedly used as a makeshift hospital and perhaps morgue? There are also stories of a servant child falling to her death in a well and a young boy who died of the plague whose body was buried within the walls to avoid detection of the family by British soldiers.

Rarely does a historic house have so many rumored legends attached to it. Despite a lack of recorded history to validate many of the claims of murder and mayhem, the legends offer as good an explanation as any for the hauntings believed to occur at the Conference House. Today, the house and grounds are owned by the City of New York but operated and maintained by the Conference House Association, with the financial assistance of the Department of Cultural Affairs, the Parks Department, the Staten Island borough president, COHASI, the Historic House Trust, and the Conference House Association's membership and auxiliary, among others. It's truly a community effort to keep the historic property available for many future generations to enjoy.

Doll of Doom

Long ago, in a mansion overlooking the Kill van Kull channel near the Bayonne Bridge, rumor has it that a woman was murdered with a doll's head that was rammed down her throat. And if that isn't horrific enough, her killer, who was never found, was believed to be the vengeful spirit of a circus freak who had hanged herself in jail several years earlier.

It all began in the mid-1860s, when Ada Danforth and the diminutive Fanchon Moncare were making regular trips between their home in Paris and their summer home on Staten Island, near the site of the old Bergen Point Ferry. To customs personnel and passengers, the two seemed likable enough—a well-dressed nanny with her friendly and courteous little charge. The child, Fanchon, was well spoken for one so young, and though she seemed wise beyond her age in that sense, she never let go of the doll she held tightly to her chest at all times. To outside appearances, the doll was nothing more than her security blanket. But what customs officials and neighbors in Port Richmond wouldn't learn for some time was that the girl was actually a woman—a 46-year-old former circus midget with a penchant for stealing jewels. Her real name was Estelle Ridley, and Ada Danforth was her accomplice. The women were jewel thieves who smuggled jewels and stolen cash between Paris and New York City by hiding it inside Fanchon's doll's head. The customs officials never considered that the innocent, childlike Fanchon was a criminal, so they never thought to search the doll's head.

Once here in the States, the women felt secure with their secret, because they paid their "dues" to members of the infamous Tweed Ring, the corrupt and grossly influential city officials who garnered more than $200 million from the city coffers between 1865 and 1871. The ring included newspapers and city officials, as well as judges and district attorneys. William Marcy "Boss" Tweed was at the helm of Tammany Hall, the Democratic headquarters that was instrumental in controlling New York City politics at the time by strong-arm, and often illegal, tactics. Like many other criminals operating in New York City back then, Ada Danforth and Estelle Ridley simply paid the massive Tweed Ring a required fee to look the other way so that they could continue their illegal activities while living lavishly in Staten Island. At the time, most New Yorkers were unaware of Tweed's activities or the fact that he was nearly bankrupting the city's treasury. The public was too enthralled with his lofty status. For a time, he could do no wrong. A *New York Times* article from December 28, 1870, before the ball was dropped on his organization, describes a large diamond pin valued at $15,500 at the time that Tweed received from his adoring friends. "It will no doubt cast a reflection of light upon the Tammany Party that will dazzle the eyes of the Young Democracy, and blind the Republicans by a Democratic victory in 1872," the article said. Could the friends that bestowed the pin to Tweed have been the jewel-stealing partners, Ridley and Danforth?

Estelle Ridley, when she wasn't disguised as Fanchon Moncare, was about as unscrupulous a character as you'd ever meet. She was promiscuous, hot-tempered, and wicked, and she often drank and gambled away her considerable wealth at the racetrack, knowing she could always get more where that came from. The racetrack is where Ridley met Magda Hamilton, and after a brief conversation, she realized the two women could benefit from each other. Both had connections to the Tweed Ring, Hamilton on a more intimate level than Ridley, and they both were up for the idea of a partnership in crime. They left for Illinois against the wishes of Ada Danforth, who tried to tell Ridley she would regret the unfamiliar partnership with Hamilton. The duo robbed a widowed old man of $350,000. When they returned to Staten Island, Ridley refused to give Hamilton her fair share, claiming that the burglary was her idea so she should get most. All she was willing to give Hamilton was $5,000. It was a mistake that would seal Ridley's fate—and Hamilton's. Hamilton stormed out of the mansion, telling Ridley she hadn't seen the last of her.

As summer came to an end that year, Danforth and Ridley returned to France. Then one night, the very wealthy Vicomte de Point Talbiere was beaten to death and robbed at an opera house in Marseilles by a man Ridley and Danforth had hired to do the deed. The investigation was sure to lead to them, as the women had been seen in public with the murdered man shortly before he was killed. With murder on their hands and a doll's head filled with a fortune in jewels, the women knew they had to return quickly to New York, where they were sure they would be shielded by Tweed's ring from authorities bent on tracking them down.

But they were wrong. As the ferry docked and the women—pretending to be a nanny and child, as always—disembarked, they were apprehended by several police officers who had been tipped off about the women's illegal affairs by none other than Magda Hamilton. At the trial, Ada Danforth offered information about the inner workings of the Tweed Ring and the money bribes they were forced to pay to continue their activities, in hopes of being granted a more lenient sentence. Her insights and accusations certainly added fuel to the fire of the crumbling ring after it was disclosed that the ring had nearly bankrupted the city. Tweed was eventually sentenced to prison for his crimes of corruption and sued by the state of New York for the money he had stolen as head of Tammany Hall. He died in prison in 1876.

Danforth was sentenced to twenty years as an accomplice, and Ridley was sentenced to life in prison for her part. Danforth's cooperation at the trial, especially her insider information about the Tweed Ring, enabled her to be paroled after just three years. When she was released, she tapped into a small fortune still in her bank account that hadn't been confiscated, and she was able to meld back into society, living well for the rest of her life.

Estelle Ridley's house on Staten Island was sold to her archenemy, Magda Hamilton, who changed her name to Mrs. Dartway Crawley and claimed to be a widow. She lived unassumingly in the house, which became known as Crawley Mansion for a number of years, smug in her knowledge that she had gotten her "fair share" from Ridley after all. But one night someone entered her house, though there were no signs of forced entry, and killed Hamilton. When the police found her body, her jaw was locked wide open, and a look of unimaginable terror was frozen on her face. She had choked on her own blood that was caused by violent trauma to her throat from a large object. Several pieces of doll's hair were said to be in her mouth, though no sign of an actual doll or murder weapon was ever found.

The woman had visited the police station just the day before her murder, very upset at having seen Estelle Ridley at the foot of her bed the previous night. When the police informed the distraught woman that Ridley had hanged herself in her jail cell years before, Hamilton made a hasty decision to leave town the next morning and go to England to escape the vengeful ghost she felt certain was stalking her. But the next morning never came for her. Legend has it that Ridley's ghost stuffed a phantom doll's head down Hamilton's throat . . . assuring that she would never again say something that would get someone into the kind of trouble that she'd gotten Ridley.

And on that note, I bid you good night . . . sleep tight.

Bibliography

Books

Barr, Lockwood. *A Brief, but Most Complete & True Account of the Settlement of the Ancient Town of Pelham, Westchester County, State of New York Known One Time Well & Favourably as The Lordshipp & Manour of Pelham. Also the Story of the Three Modern Villages Called the Pelhams.* Petersburg, VA: Dietz Press, 1946.

Bartell, Jan Bryant. *Spindrift: Spray from a Psychic Sea.* Portland, OR: Hawthorne Books, 1974.

Blackman, W. Haden. *The Field Guide to North American Hauntings.* NY: Three River Press, 1998.

Bord, Jane, and Colin Bord. *The Bigfoot Casebook.* Mechanicsburg, PA: Stackpole Books, 1982.

Brady, Mathew. *The Gallery of Illustrious Americans.* New York: Self-published, 1850.

Croffut, William Augustus. *The Vanderbilts and the Story of Their Fortune.* Chicago: Belford, Clarke, and Company, 1886.

Hauck, Dennis William. *Haunted Places: The National Directory: Ghostly Abodes, Sacret Sites, UFO Landings and Other Supernatural Locations.* New York: Penguin, 2002.

Howard, S. B. *Strange but True New York City.* Guilford, CT: Insiders' Guide— Globe Pequot Press, 2005.

Irving, Washington [Diedrich Knickerbocker, pseud.]. *A History of New York, from the Beginning of the World to the End of the Dutch Dynasty.* Vol. 1. New York: Inskeep and Bradford, 1809.

Kaplan, Stephen, and Carol Kane. *Vampires Are.* Palm Springs, CA: ETC Publications, 1984.

Macken, Lynda Lee. *Haunted History of Staten Island.* NJ: Black Cat Press, 2000.

McCabe, James Dabney [Edward Winslow Martin, pseud.]. *The Secrets of the Great City: A Work Descriptive of the Virtues and Vices, the Mysteries, Miseries, and Crimes of New York City.* Philadelphia, PA: Jones Brothers & Co., 1868.

Mowatt, Anna Cora. *Autobiography of an Actress; or, Eight Years on the Stage.* Boston, MA: Ticknor, Reed, and Fields, 1854.

Revai, Cheri. *Haunted Massachusetts: Ghosts and Strange Phenomena of the Bay State.* Mechanicsburg, PA: Stackpole Books, 2005.

────── *Haunted New York: Ghosts and Strange Phenomena of the Empire State.* Mechanicsburg, PA: Stackpole Books, 2005.

Rice, Ann. *Complete Vampire Chronicles.* NY: Ballantine Books, 1993.

Bolton, Robert Jr. *A History of the County of Westchester, from Its First Settlement to the Present Time.* Vol. I. New York: Alexander S. Gould, 1848.

────── *The History of The Several Towns, Manors, and Patents of the County of Westchester, from Its First Settlement to the Present Time Carefully Revised by its Author.* Vol. 2. New York: Chas. F. Roper, 1881.

Schlosser, S. E. *Spooky New York.* Guilford, CT: Globe Pequot, 2005.

Taylor, Troy. *No Rest for the Wicked.* Decatur, IL: Whitechapel Press, 2001.

Van der Donck, Adriaen. *A Description of the New Netherlands.* 1841. English translation edited by Thomas F. O'Donnell. Reprint. Syracuse, NY: Syracuse University Press, 1968.

Whyte, William H. *WPA Guide to New York City: The Federal Writer's Project Guide to 1930s New York.* 1939. Reprint. New York: Pantheon Books, 1982.

Wicker, Christine. *Lily Dale: The True Story of the Town That Talks to the Dead.* NY: HarperCollins, 2004.

Magazine Articles

(in order by story)

"Miracle in the Bronx." *Time,* 24 July 1939.

"Shrine in the Bronx." *Time,* 26 November 1945.

"Tiffany Revisited." *Time,* 16 February 1959.

"Bum." *Time,* 27 April 1931.

"Living It Up." *Time,* 13 April 1962.

"Religion & Finance." *Time,* 25 March 1929.

"Fire on Air." *Time,* 15 August 1938.

Swan, Annalyn. "Talking Walls." *Time,* 27 August 1979.

Hirshey, Gerri. "The Cradle of Our Religious Freedom." *Parade,* 17 April 2005.

Newspaper Sources

(in order by story)

Twomey, Bill. "Tales of Headless Indians at the Haunted Cedar Knoll." *Bronx Times Reporter,* 9 May 2002.

"Doings in Lorillard Lane: Helmets Battered and Clothes Torn by a Bronx "What-Is-It." *New York Times,* 22 June 1904.

"Griffins Frightened Away." *Brooklyn Daily Eagle,* 23 October 1901, page 6.

"100th Year Marked by Brooklyn Church." *New York Times,* 23 October 1941.

Bibliography

"All in White." *Brooklyn Daily Eagle,* 12 August 1890, page 6.

"Many Saw Her." *Brooklyn Daily Eagle,* 14 August 1890, page 2.

"The Sin of Telling Fortunes." *Brooklyn Daily Eagle,* 20 June 1897, page 6.

Gordon, David. "Whatever Else Changes in Brooklyn, the Traditional Ghosts Remain." *New York Times,* 18 May 1975.

"History of Flatbush." *Brooklyn Standard Union,* 27 August 1928.

"A Flatbush Legend: The Ghost Story of the Mansion in Melrose Park." *Brooklyn Daily Eagle,* 22 June 1884.

"A Tale of Melrose Hall." *Brooklyn Daily Eagle,* 9 March 1890, page 17.

"Another Long Island Discovery." *Brooklyn Daily Eagle,* 27 December 1893, page 4.

"The Ghost of Melrose Hall." *Brooklyn Daily Eagle,* 13 October 1895, page 8.

"Melrose Hall Sold." *Brooklyn Daily Eagle,* 9 April 1901, page 5.

"An Aerial Mystery." *New York Times,* 12 September 1880.

"A Brewery Burned." *Brooklyn Daily Eagle,* 26 December 1874, page 3.

"An Establishment Which Has Emphasized Itself." *Brooklyn Daily Eagle,* 29 July 1888, page 10.

"Noted Men Go There." *Brooklyn Daily Eagle,* 26 October 1890, page 19.

"Adams Holds the Reins." *Brooklyn Daily Eagle,* 15 January 1893, page 16.

"Piel Bros." (advertisement) *Brooklyn Daily Eagle,* 29 September 1895, page 21.

"Called It a Haunted House." *Brooklyn Daily Eagle,* 9 October 1895, page 12.

"Enlarge Beer Plant." *New York Times,* 25 May 1937.

"Bert and Harry Brew Last Batch." *New York Times,* 21 September 1973.

"News Summary and Index, Saturday, September 22, 1973—Correction." *New York Times,* 22 September 1973.

"Killed Two." *Brooklyn Daily Eagle,* 16 December 1891, page 4.

"The Borchinsky Double Murder." *Brooklyn Daily Eagle,* 16 December 1891, page 6

"Lowly Burial: The Borchinsky Funeral Held in a Stable." *Brooklyn Daily Eagle,* 18 December 1891, page 6.

"Simon Free: Justice Walsh Discharges the Borchinsky Suspect." *Brooklyn Daily Eagle,* 19 December 1891, page 6.

"Not For Money: An Arrest in the Borchinsky Murder Case." *Brooklyn Daily Eagle,* 15 January 1892, page 6.

"Wants to Wed—but a Terrible Tragedy Evidently Haunts Him." *Brooklyn Daily Eagle,* 22 April 1892, page 6.

"Waiting to See a Ghost: Queer Spectacle at the Scene of the Boschinsky Murders." *Brooklyn Daily Eagle,* 3 July 1892, page 20.

"Ida Is a Great Talker—and She Isn't Afraid of Having Her Throat Cut." *Brooklyn Daily Eagle,* 6 June 1894, page 1.

"Accused of Double Murder: Did Max Blatchinsky Butcher His Wife and Child?" *Brooklyn Daily Eagle,* 16 June 1894, page 12.

"How Boschinsky Was Caught." *Brooklyn Daily Eagle,* 17 June 1894, page 24.

"Boschinsky's Arrest." *Brooklyn Daily Eagle,* 18 June 1894, page 6.

"The Blackinsky Murder Case." *Brooklyn Daily Eagle,* 19 June 1894, page 1.

"Kirchner Was Not Merciful: Judge Moore Imposes a Heavy Sentence on Wife Killer." *Brooklyn Daily Eagle*, 30 September 1894.

"Says He Is a Murderer: John C. Matthews Reports the Capture of a Criminal." *Brooklyn Daily Eagle*, 14 September 1895.

Ray, C. Clairborne. "Q&A: Ball Lightning." *New York Times*, 8 August 1995.

"Freaks of the Lightning." *New York Times*, 25 July 1897.

"Rain, Hail, and Fireballs." *New York Times*, 24 July 1897.

"Storm Strikes the City." *New York Times*, 24 July 1897.

"Violent Remedy Cured Him." *New York Times*, 24 July 1897.

"Died from Storm Fright." *New York Times*, 25 July 1897.

"New Apartments on the West Side." *New York Times*, 13 May 1956.

"City to Lose First Apartments as 'Stuyvesant's Folly' Fades." *New York Times*, 22 September 1957.

Ennis, Thomas W. "City Soon to Lose First Apartments." *New York Times*, 22 September 1957.

Bartnett, Edmond J. "Stuyvesant Square Keeps Its Quiet Dignity Despite New Construction." *New York Times*, 4 November 1962.

"Stuyvesant Sq. Retaining Charm." *New York Times*, 4 November 1962.

"C.B.S. to Rename Studio Ed Sullivan Theater Dec. 10." *New York Times*, 20 November 1967.

"Beatles Prepare for Their Debut." *New York Times*, 9 February 1964.

"Hammerstein's Sister Visits Theatre." *New York Times*, 9 December 1927.

"New Name Is Given to Hammerstein's." *The New York Times*, 5 August 1931.

"Ed Sullivan Is Dead at 73; Charmed Millions on TV." *New York Times*, 14 October 1974.

"Lieut. Alfred A. Stokes: Inhalators Fail to Aid Fireman Stricken by Heart Attack." *New York Times*, 11 August 1939.

"Four Murderers Hanged." *New York Times*, 24 August 1889.

"Charged with Abduction." *New York Times*, 10 July 1887.

"He Killed Her." *New York Times*, 18 July 1888.

"F.Y.I. Firehouse Apparitions." *New York Times*, 14 February 1999.

Spet, David. "Patrol That 'Puts Out the Water' May Be Dissolved." *Villager*, Vol. 76, No. 12. Retrieved 26 February 2007.

Berger, Meyer. "There's Still a Ghost of a Chance Old Merchant's House Near the Bowery May Be Haunted." *New York Times*, 27 November 1953.

"Old Tredwell Home Opened as Museum." *New York Times*, 12 May 1936.

KilGannon, Corey. "Making It Work; Tracking Gertrude Tredwell's Ghost." *New York Times*, 25 October 1998.

Dunning, Jennifer. "A Skeleton Key to Halloween Tricks and Treats." *New York Times*, 30 October 1981.

Yarnell, Kolby. "30 Years of Keeping Watch over Ghosts and Crypts at St. Mark's Church." *New York Sun*, 17 November 2004.

"New York Fire Kills 148: Girl Victims Leap to Death from Factory." *Chicago Sunday Tribune*, 26 March 1911.

Rosenbloom, Stephanie. "Some Buyers Regret Not Asking: Anyone Die Here?" *New York Times*, 30 April 2006.

Bibliography

Shipp, E. R. "Mark Twain's Death Recalled on W. 10th St." *New York Times*, 22 April 1980.

"Died—Lee." *New York Times*, 3 December 1899.

"Found in a Lonely Lane: A Young Woman Shoots Herself in Central Park." *New York Times*, 7 September 1885.

Price, Claire. "Indian Magic Again Puzzles Scientists." *New York Times*, 20 October 1935.

"Supernatural?" *New York Times*, 24 September 1935.

LeDuff, Charlie. "They Heard, They Came, They Await the End." *New York Times*, 23 March 1997.

Kilgannon, Corey. "Visions of Doom Endure in Queens: Prophecy, and a Rift, at a Shrine." *New York Times*, 9 October 2003.

Kaiser, Charles. "Ban on Outdoor Prayer Sessions in Queens Is Sought." *New York Times*, 2 April 1975.

Cooper, Michael. "Church Says Burglar Sought Saint's Icon." *New York Times*, 12 August 1998.

Ojito, Mirta. "Relic Brings Clout and Miracle Seekers to a Queens Church." *New York Times*, 23 December 1996.

"Insurance Suit Is Filed over Weeping Icon." *New York Times*, 16 July 1994.

Stanley, Alessandra. "Story of the Weeping Icon Divides Greek Orthodoxy." *New York Times*, 1 January 1992.

Lorch, Donatella. "Queens Church Robbed of 'Weeping' Icon." *New York Times*, 24 December 1991.

"A Haunted Woman." *Brooklyn Eagle*, 27 July 1884.

"A Monosyllabic Ghost." *Brooklyn Eagle*, 28 July 1884.

"Posses of Men Hunting in Vain a Ghost on Long Island." *New York Times*, 27 July 1884.

"A Hungry Ghost." *New York Times*, 30 July 1884.

"Following an Elusive Voice." *New York Times*, 27 July 1884.

"The Wild Man Still Visible." *Brooklyn Eagle*, 12 December 1885.

"It's Tall, It Has Wavy Red Hair and Chinese Keep Hunting for It." *New York Times*, 5 January 1980.

"Police at Mineola Hunt Ape-like Animal." *New York Times*, 30 June 1931.

Goff, Liz. "Queens' Ghosts Are Here All Year Round." *Queens Gazette*, 1 November 2006.

"An Old Landmark Sold." *New York Times*, 1 April 1886.

Gentilviso, Richard. "City Takes Ownership of Bowne House." *Queens Gazette*, 17 December 2003.

Fried, Joseph P. "A Clash over Revival of a Queens Landmark." *New York Times*, 19 February 1989.

Belluck, Pam. "A New Star in Constellation of Art's Giants; Queens Landmark Wins a Coveted Cultural Title." *New York Times*, 21 May 1996.

"Drama in the Flushing Town Hall: Actors Find Home in a Landmark." *New York Times*, 21 November 1976.

"Kingsland Homestead Now a Museum." *New York Times*, 25 March 1973.

McShane, Larry. "Houdini Poisoned? Kin Wants Exhumation." *Associated Press*, 23 March 2007.

"Houdini's Body Gets Here Today." *New York Times*, 2 November 1926.

Murphy, Dean E. "With Police Help, a Bust of Houdini Reappears." *New York Times*, 10 March 2002.

Dowd, Maureen. "Is New York Too Scary Even for Its Ghosts?" *New York Times*, 31 October 1985.

Johnston, Laurie and Susan Heller Anderson. "New York Day by Day; Trick on Cemetery Thieves." *New York Times*, 18 August 1983.

"Vandals Destroy Houdini Grave Bust." *New York Times*, 10 April 1975.

Martin, Douglas. "Resting in Comparative Peace; To Keep Vandals Away, Houdini's Grave Is Closed for Halloween." *New York Times*, 30 October 1995.

Grimes, William. "Grading the Gothic in Gotham." *New York Times*, 30 October 1992.

Mittelbach, Margaret and Michael Crewdson. "To Die For: Painting the Town Red, and the Capes and Nails Black." *New York Times*, 24 November 2000.

McGuire, Stephen. "Haunted Happenings: Highlights for Halloween in Queens." *Queens Tribune*, 24 October 2002.

Azzara, Mike. "With the Help of Wagner College's President, Augustinian Academy Alumni Hope to Create a Permanent Hall of Memories, Scholarship Fund." *Staten Island Advance*, January 15, 2006.

Young, Deborah. "From Ruins of a School, Intriguing Relics." *Staten Island Advance*. 21 March 2006.

Press Clips. "Lament for a Lost Landmark." *Staten Island Advance*, 8 March, 2006.

Destefano, Anthony M. "Feds: 'Haunted' House Scene of Grisly Mob Murder." *Newsday*, 12 May 2006.

Rashbaum, William K. "Grisly Mob Killing at S.I. Mansion Is Detailed." *New York Times*, 12 May 2006.

Seaberg, Maureen, and Robert F. Moore. "Mansion Mystery." *New York Daily News*, 6 April 2006.

O'Shea, Karen. "Murder Stuns Man Restoring Kreischer Mansion." *Staten Island Advance*, 12 May 2006.

Patrick, Reginald. "Search at Mansion Eerily Familiar." *Staten Island Advance*, 7 April 2006.

Porpora, Tracey. "What's Haunting the Conference House?" *Staten Island Advance*, 5 August 1999.

"The Ring and Its Friends." *New York Times*, 28 December 1870.

Online Sources
(in order by story)

"New York City." *Wikipedia*. Retrieved 29 April 2007.
en.wikipedia.org/wiki/New_york_city.

"New Amsterdam." *Wikipedia*. Retrieved 15 May 2007.
en.wikipedia.org/wiki/New_Amsterdam.

Bibliography

"New Netherland." *Wikipedia.* Retrieved 15 May 2007.
en.wikipedia.org/wiki/New_Netherland.

"New York City." *New York City Region Communities.* Retrieved 2 May 2007.
iloveny.com/ourcities/CityProfile/NYCCommunities.aspx.

"History of New York State Before 1900." *History—I Love New York—
The Official New York State Tourism Website.* Retrieved 2 May 2007.
iloveny.com/AboutNY/History.aspx.

"The Bronx." *Wikipedia.* Retrieved 29 April 2007.
en.wikipedia.org/wiki/The_Bronx.

"The Most Haunted Building on Campus." *Fordhamensis: The Most Haunted
Building on Campus.* Retrieved 16 January 2007.
community.livejournal.com/fordhamensis/237113.html.

"Queen's Court Residential College." *Fordham University—The Office of
Residential Life at Rose Hill.* Retrieved 16 January 2007.
www.fordham.edu/student_affairs/residential_life/rose_hill/residence
halls/queens...

"Martyr's Court." *Fordham University—The Office of Residential Life at Rose
Hill.* Retrieved 16 January 2007. www.fordham.edu/student_affairs/
residential_life/rose_hill/residence_halls/martyrs_...

"Fordham University." *Ghost Stories, Hauntings, Supernatural Tales.*
Retrieved 14 January 2007.
originaltales.com/urban/Listings.php?City = B&State = NY&Type = 3.

Weil, Jennifer. "Seeking Miracles in City Water." *Columbia News Service.*
Retrieved 28 January 2007.
www.jrn.columbia.edu/studentwork/cns/2002-04-03/322.asp.

"Miracle in the Bronx." *Time Archive* online. Published 24 July 1939.
Retrieved 28 January 2007. www.time.com/time/magazine/
article/0,9171,771685,00.html.

"Shrine in the Bronx." *Time Archive* online. Published 26 November 1945.
Retrieved 21 January 2007. www.time.com/time/magazine/
article/0,9171,776401,00.html.

"The Boy Who Saw the Virgin." *Visions of Jesus Christ.com.* Retrieved
21 January 2007. www.visionsofjesuschrist.com/weeping278.htm.

Twomey, Bill. "Tales of Headless Indians at the Haunted Cedar Knoll."
Bronx Times Reporter, 9 May 2002. Retrieved 16 January 2007.
www.bronxmall.com/cult/twomey/cedarknoll.html.

"Pelham Bay Park." *New York City Department of Parks & Recreation.*
Retrieved 21 January 2007.
www.nycgovparks.org/sub_your_park/vt_pelham_bay_park/vt_
pelham_bay_park.html.

Bell, Blake A. "Pelham's Ghosts, Goblins and Legends." *Historic Pelham.*
Retrieved 16 May 2007. www.historicpelham.com/BellGhostsArticle.htm.

Bell, Blake. "1854 Advertisement for the Sale of the Old Stone House at 463
First Avenue in Pelham." *Historic Pelham.* Blog dated 17 March 2006.
Retrieved 22 January 2007. historicpelham.blogspot.com/2006/03/
1854-advertisement-for-sale-of-old.html.

"Pelville." *Pelham, New York, Landmarks.* Retrieved 22 January 2007.
www.pelhamny.com/landmarks/pelville.html.

"Adriaen van der Donck." *Wikipedia.* Retrieved 23 January 2007.
en.wikipedia.org/w/index.php?title = Adriaen_van_der_Donck.

Van der Donck, Adriaen. "Description of the New Netherlands"
(seventeenth-century document). *Cornell Library New York State
Historical Literature.* Retrieved 22 January 2007. historical.library
.cornell.edu/cgi-bin/cul.nys/docviewer?did + nys161&seq = 7&frames...

"Brooklyn." *Wikipedia.* Retrieved 29 April 2007.
en.wikipedia.org/wiki/Brooklyn.

"Modern Improvements and Gentrification." *Bedford-Stuyvesant, Brooklyn—
Wikipedia.* Retrieved 18 February 2007. en.wikipedia.org/wiki/
Bedford-Stuyvesant,_Brooklyn.

"Stuyvesant Heights." *Stuyvesant Heights, Brooklyn.* Retrieved 18 February
2007. www.brooklyn.net/neighborhoods/Stuyvesant_heights.html.

"Bedford-Stuyvesant." *Bedford-Stuy Neighborhood Guide.* Retrieved
18 February 2007. www.nestseekers.com/Guides/Neighborhood/2004.

"Tales of a Haunted Most Holy Trinity." *Most Holy Trinity Church:
Haunted Trinity.* Retrieved 30 January 2007.
www.mhtbrooklyn.org/en_hauntedtrinity.htm.

Most Holy Trinity Roman Catholic Church. Home page. Retrieved 18 February
2007. www.mhtbrooklyn.org/.

"History." *Most Holy Trinity Church: History.* Retrieved 30 January 2007.
www.mhtbrooklyn.org/en_history.htm.

"About Pool Parties." *The Pool Parties.* Retrieved 18 February 2007.
www.thepoolparties.com/about.php.

Villella, Dominick. "McCarren Park Swimming Pool." *Paranormal Investigation of NYC.* Retrieved 18 February 2007. www.paranormal-nyc.com/.

Carlson, Jen. "McCarren Park Pool Controversy." *Gothamist.* Retrieved 30
January 2007. www.gothamist.com/archives/2006/05/25/mccarren.php.

Cosgrove, Julie, and Emily Kaufman. "Buried New York: Small Spirits."
Time Out NY Kids. Retrieved 30 January 2007.
www.tonykids.com/features/8k8.ft.buried.html.

"McCarren Park." *McCarren Park—Historical Sign.* Retrieved 30 January
2007. www.nycgovparks.org/sub_your_park/historical_signs/hs
_historical_sign.php?id = 200.

"Williamsburg, Brooklyn." *Wikipedia.* Retrieved 30 January 2007.
en.wikipedia.org/wiki/Williamsburg,_Brooklyn.

"News from the Tenement—November 2006." *Lower East Side Tenement
Museum.* Retrieved 9 February 2007.
www.tenement.org/newsarchive_nov06.html.

"New York Penal Law Section 165.35—Fortune Telling." *New York Penal
Law—Legal Research.* Retrieved 9 February 2007. law.onecle.com/
new-york/penal/PEN0165.35_165.35.html.

Kurtz, Paul. "The New Paranatural Paradigm." *Committee for Skeptical Inquiry.*
Retrieved 18 May 2007. www.csicop.org/si/2000-11/paranatural.html.

Bibliography

Lewy, Guenter. "The Travail of the Gypsies." *The National Interest*. Fall 1999.
    Retrieved 18 May 2007. www.cianet.org/olj/ni/ni_99leg01.html.
"Fortune-telling." *Wikipedia*. Retrieved 18 May 2007.
    en.wikipedia.org/wiki/Fortune-telling.
"Tiffanys Revisited." *Time* magazine online news archive. 16 February 1959.
    Retrieved 8 February 2007. www.time.com/time/magazine/article/
    0,9171,894199,00.html.
"A Romance of Melrose Abbey." *Rambles of Old Brooklyn*. Retrieved
    8 February 2007. www.bklyn-genealogy-info.com/Town/Rambles/
    MelroseAbbey2.html.
"William Axtell 1720-1795 Landowner." *Biographical Sketches of Wealthy
    Men of the Colonial Era in New York*. Retrieved 3 February 2007.
    www.thehistorybox.com/ny_city/society/printerfriendly/nycity
    _society_bios_colonial_article0005.htm.
"Beauty in Diversity." *Flatbush, Long Island*. Retrieved 3 February 2007.
    www.longislandexchange.com/brooklynqueens/Flatbush.html.
"When Flatbush Was Greenwich . . ." *Flatbush 2*. Retrieved 31 January 2007.
    home.att.net/ ~ ebasics/flatbush2.html.
Axtell, Carson A. "Gleanings from England and Elsewhere." *Axtell
    Genealogy*. Published 1945. Retrieved 3 February 2007.
    www.axtellfamily.org/axgenea/axglean.html.
"Bum." *Time* magazine. 27 April 1931. Retrieved 18 February 2007.
    www.time.com/time/magazine/article/0,9171,741531,00.html.
Jones, Meg. "Healer's Faith." *Milwaukee Journal Sentinel*. (JSOnline.)
    Posted 21 December 2004. Retrieved 11 January 2007.
    www.jsonline.com/story/index.aspx?id = 286243.
"Do You Believe in Miracles?" *Unexplained Mysteries*. Posted online
    27 December 2005. Retrieved 11 January 2007.
    www.unexplained-mysteries.com/viewnews.php?id = 58053.
Wagner, Stephen. "Astonishing Accounts of People Who Fly—With Wings
    or Without." *Unsolved: Flying Humanoids*. Retrieved 9 February 2007.
    paranormal.about.com/cs/humanenigmas/a/aa082503.htm.
"Flying Humanoids." *Unknown Creatures*. Retrieved 30 January 2007.
    www.unknown-creatures.com/flying-humanoids.html.
"315 Liberty Avenue—Incredible Leasing with an Option to Buy."
    Halstead Property. Retrieved 7 February 2007.
    www.halstead.com/detail.aspx?id = 1153664.
"Piels Brewery." *The East New York Project*. Retrieved 4 February 2007.
    www.tapeshare.com/Piels.html.
"A Brooklyn Brewery's Brothers Act Had Right Spiel for Fans of Piels."
    Times Newsweekly Online. 7 February 2002. Retrieved 6 February 2007.
    www.timesnewsweekly.com/Archives2002/Jan.-.
"Manhattan." *Wikipedia*. Retrieved 29 April 2007.
    en.wikipedia.org/wiki/Manhattan.
Kruszelnicki, Karl S. "Ball Lightning." *Great Moments in Science*. Retrieved
    16 March 2007. www.abc.net.au/science/k2/moments/s1217660.htm.

"Ball Lightning." *Wikipedia*. Retrieved 16 March 2007. en.wikipedia.org/wiki/Ball_lightning.

"Ball Lightning Page." *High Voltage Mystery*. Retrieved 16 March 2007. amasci.com/tesla/ballgtn.html.

"Now You See It, Soon You Won't." *Animal*. Retrieved 22 February 2007. animalnewyork.com/2006/05/now_you_see_it_soon_you_wont_1.php.

Abbott, Berenice. "Oldest Apartment House in New York City." *Museum of the City of New York*. Retrieved 22 February 2007. www.mcny.org/collections/abbott/a062.htm.

"Ed Sullivan Theater." *Wikipedia*. Retrieved 27 February 2007. en.wikipedia.org/wiki/Ed_Sullivan_Theater.

"915—Ed Sullivan Theater Investigation." *Paranormal NYC—Investigations*. Retrieved 17 January 2007. www.paranormal-nyc.com/915.html.

"Station House 2." *New York Board of Fire Underwriters*. Retrieved 26 February 2007. www.simplywebandgraphicdesign.com/nybfu/firepatrol_html/station2.htm.

"About Us." *New York Board of Fire Underwriters*. Retrieved 26 February 2007. www.simplywebandgraphicdesign.com/nybfu/firepatrol_html/aboutus.htm.

Pollak, Michael. "Entry from May 28, 2006: Manhattan Solstice (Manhattanhenge or Sensational Sunset)." *The Big Apple*. Retrieved 2 May 2007. www.barrypopik.com/index.php/new_york_city/entry/manhattan_solstice_manhattanhenge_or_sensational_sunset/.

"Manhattanhenge." *Wikipedia*. Retrieved 2 May 2007. en.wikipedia.org/wiki/Manhattanhenge.

"Sunset on 34th Street Along the Manhattan Grid." *Natural History* magazine. Retrieved 2 May 2007. www.naturalhistorymag.com/city_of_stars/19_sunset_34th.html.

"Stonehenge." *Crystalinks*. Retrieved 3 May 2007. www.crystalinks.com/Stonehenge.html.

"Merchant's House Museum." *Answers.com*. Retrieved 27 February 2007. www.answers.com/topic/merchant-s-house-museum.

"A Haunted Tale of Broken Love." *AM New York*. Retrieved 10 March 2007. www.amny.com/entertainment/nyc-haunted,0,7442732.

"Merchant's House Museum." *Merchants House Museum*. Retrieved 27 February 2007. www.merchantshouse.com/.

"History." *St. Mark's Church in-the-Bowery*. Retrieved 12 March 2007. www.stmarkschurch-in-the-bowery.com/?q=node/40.

"St. Mark's Church." *Everything2*. Retrieved 12 March 2007. everything2.com/index.pl?node_id=835087.

"St. Patrick's Cathedral, New York." *Answers.com*. Retrieved 12 March 2007. www.answers.com/topic/st-patrick-s-cathedral-new-york.

"St. Patrick's Old Cathedral (RC)." *New York Architecture Images*. Retrieved 12 March 2007. www.nyc-architecture.com/SOH/SOH038.htm.

"St. Patrick's Old Cathedral, New York." *Wikipedia*. Retrieved 12 March 2007. en.wikipedia.org/wiki/St._Patrick's_Old_Cathedral,_NewYork.

Bibliography

"Saint Patrick's Old Cathedral." *Home Page.* Retrieved 12 March 2007.
www.oldsaintpatricks.com/osp_contents.html.

"Trinity Church Cemetery." *Answers.com.* Retrieved 12 March 2007.
www.answers.com/topic/trinity-church-cemetery.

"History of NYU." *New York University.* Retrieved 14 January 2007.
www.nyu.edu/about/history.html.

"University Facts." *New York University.* Retrieved 19 March 2007.
www.nyu.edu/about/facts.html.

"New York University." *Wikipedia.* Retrieved 19 March 2007.
en.wikipedia.org/wiki/New_York_University.

"NYS—West Village: Brown Building—Triangle Shirtwaist Factory/
Fire Plaques." *Flickr.* Retrieved 19 March 2007. www.flickr.com/
photos/wallyg/371357205/.

"Triangle Fire: March 25, 1911." *Painting the Town—Museum of the City
of New York.* Retrieved 19 March 2007.
www.mcny.org/collections/painting/pttcat58.htm.

"Triangle Shirtwaist Factory Building." *Shirtwaist Factory—NRHP Travel
Itinerary.* Retrieved 19 March 2007.
www.cr.nps.gov/nr/travel/pwwmh/ny30.htm.

"The Haunted New York Experience." *Ghosts of New York Walking Tours.*
Retrieved 18 May 2007. www.ghostsofny.com/tours.html.

Dyba, Beth. "NYU Ghost Stories: Students Share Their Scariest Tales." Washington Square News. Posted 1 January 1997. Retrieved 14 January 2007.
media.www.nyunews.com/media/storage/paper869/news/1997/01/01/
UndefinedSection/Nyu-Ghost.Stories.Students.Share.Their.Scariest
.T-2395849.shtml#more.

Slepoy, Natasha. "Brittany." *Washington Square News.* Posted 3 March 2005.
Retrieved 14 January 2007.
media.www.nyunews.com/media/storage/paper869/news/2005/03/03/
UndefinedSection/Brittany-2388184.shtml.

Brabson, Kristine. "Histories Haunt Traditional-Style Dorms." Washington
Square News. Posted 1 January 1997. Retrieved 14 January 2007.
media.www.nyunews.com/media/storage/paper869/news/1997/01/01/
UndefinedSection/Histories.Haunt.TraditionalStyle.Dorms-2394200
.shtml.

"NYC—West Village: 14 West 10th Street." *Flickr.* Retrieved 27 February
2007. www.flickr.com/photos/wallyg/327046411/.

Gado, Mark. "A Child Not Breathing." *Court TV Crime Library.* Retrieved
27 February 2007.
www.crimelibrary.com/notorious_murders/family/lisa_steinberg/1.html.

"Wollman Rink in Central Park." *Halloween Haunts of NYC on Squidoo.*
Retrieved 10 March 2007. www.squidoo.com/HauntedNYC/.

"Wollman Rink." *Central Park Conservancy.* Retrieved 23 February 2007.
www.centralparknyc.org/virtualpark/southbend/wollmanrink.

"150 + Years of Park History." Central Park Conservancy. Retrieved 23 February 2007. www.centralparknyc.org/centralparkhistory/cp-history-150yrs.

"About Us." *St. Paul's Chapel in The NYC Insider.* Retrieved 9 February 2007. www.saintpaulschapel.org/about_us/.

"St. Paul's Chapel." *NYC Insider.* Retrieved 9 February 2007. www.theinsider.com/nyc/attractions/2st-paul.htm.

"George Frederick Cooke." *Find a Grave Memorial.* Retrieved 9 February 2007. www.findagrave.com/cgi-bin/fg.cgi?page = gr&Grid = 7938393.

"Mathew B. Brady: Civil War Photographer." *American Civil War.* Retrieved 12 February 2007. www.americanrevwar.homestead.com/files/civwar/brady.htm.

"Second Sight: The Phenomenon of Eyeless Vision." *Red Orbit News.* Retrieved 11 January 2007. www.redorbit.com/modules/news/tools.php?tool = print&id = 149258.

"Kuda Bux." *Answers.com.* Retrieved 20 March 2007. www.answers.com/Kuda % 20Bux?print = true.

"Medical Intuitive." *Answers.com.* Retrieved 20 March 2007. www.answers.com/medical % 20intuitives?print = true.

Choukri, Sam. "The Dakota and Strawberry Fields Memorial." *Bagism.* Retrieved 27 February 2007. www.bagism.com/library/nyc-sf-dakota.html.

Harry, Bill. "John Lennon in the Spirit World." *Mersey Beat.* Retrieved 27 February 2007. triumphpc.com/Mersey-beat/beatles/spirit-world.shtml.

"The Dakota." *Wikipedia.* Retrieved 27 February 2007. en.wikipedia.org/wiki/The_Dakota.

Patterson, R. Gary. "Recap: John Lennon Mysteries." *Coast to Coast AM with George Noory.* Retrieved 9 March 2007. www.coasttocoastam.com/shows/2005/12/08.html.

"Queens." *Wikipedia.* Retrieved 29 April 2007. en.wikipedia.org/wiki/Queens.

"Miraculous Photos." *St. Michael's World Apostolate.* Retrieved 31 March 2007. www.smwa.org/Documents/Miraculous_Photos/Mirac_photo _library/Document_Miraculous_Photo_Library.htm.

"Background." *St. Michael's World Apostolate.* Retrieved 31 March 2007. www.smwa.org/SMWA/Document_SMWA_background.htm.

"The Virgin Mary Appears in America." *St. Michael's World Apostolate.* Retrieved 31 March 2007. www.smwa.org/SMWA/Shrine_Guards/ Document_What_is_a_Shrine_guard.htm.

"Veronica Lueken." *Answers.com.* Retrieved 29 March 2007. www.answers.com/veronica % 20lueken.

Rutkoff, Aaron, Angela Montefinise, and Myles Gordon. "The Afterlife of Fort Totten: From Platoons to Playgrounds." *QueensTribune.com.* Retrieved 28 March 2007. www.queenstribune.com/anniversary2003/forttotten.htm.

Hampton, Matt. "Tracking Ft. Totten." *Graveyard Ghosthunters of America.* Retrieved 9 February 2007. graveyardghosthuntersofamerica.com/images/scan0006.jpg.

"Mayor Bloomberg Opens Fort Totten Park to the Public." *New York City Department of Parks and Recreation.* 13 June 2005. Retrieved 28 March

Bibliography

2007. www.nycgovparks.org/sub_newsroom/press_release/press_releases.php?id = 19541.

"Mission/History." *Bayside Historical Society Information.* Retrieved 28 March 2007. www.baysidehistorical.org/info/info.html.

"Nike Missile Battery at Fort Slocum." *Fort Totten.org.* Retrieved 28 March 2007. www.forttotten.org/Links.shtml.

"Deteriorating Civil War Landmarks in Queens to Be Rescued by Cornell Students and Other Volunteers, April 12–14." *Cornell News.* 10 April 2002. Retrieved 28 March 2007. www.news.cornell.edu/releases/April02/Ft.Totten.project.html.

"Historical Timeline." *Fort Totten.org.* Retrieved 28 March 2007. www.forttotten.org/Timeline.shtml.

"Historical." *Fort Totten.org.* Retrieved 28 March 2007. www.forttotten.org/Links.shtml.

"Fort Totten, New York." *Wikipedia.* Retrieved 9 February 2007. en.wikipedia.org/wiki/Fort_Totten,_Queens.

"Joseph Gilbert Totten." *Wikipedia.* Retrieved 28 March 2007. en.wikipedia.org/wiki/Joseph_G._Totten.

"History of Middle Village and the Lutheran Cemetery." *History of Middle Village and the Lutheran Cemetery.* Retrieved 12 February 2007. www.junipercivic.com/HistoryArticle.asp?nid = 53.

"History of Mount Olivet Cemetery." *Mount Olivet Cemetery.* Retrieved 13 February 2007. www.mountolivetcemeterynyc.com/mainframe.htm.

"Cover Story." *Southeast Queens Press.* Retrieved 26 March 2007. queenspress.com/archives/coverstories/2000/issue25/coverstory.htm.

Walsh, Kevin. "Forgotten Tour 21: Return to Flushing." *Forgotten NY.* Retrieved 26 March 2007. www.forgotten-ny.com/forgottentour21/tour21.html.

"The House: History." *Bowne House Historical Society.* Retrieved 29 March 2007. www.bownehouse.org/photo/history_p.php.

"Restoration Fact Sheet 2006." *Bowne House Historical Society.* Retrieved 29 March 2007. www.bownehouse.org/about/restoration_p.php.

"John Bowne." *Wikipedia.* Retrieved 29 March 2007. en.wikipedia.org/wiki/John_Bowne.

"March 1936: Bowne House Mary Pickford." *Greater Astoria Historical Society.* Retrieved 11 January 2007. www.astorialic.org/starjournal/1930s/1936march_p.php.

"About the Building." *Flushing Town Hall.* Retrieved 24 March 2007. www.flushingtownhall.org/visiting/building.php.

"Visiting." *Flushing Town Hall.* Retrieved 24 March 2007. www.flushingtownhall.org/visiting/index.php.

Roleke, John. "Haunted Queens." *About: New York: Queens.* Retrieved 25 March 2007. queens.about.com/b/a/214933.htm.

"Ghastly Ghosts Craft Workshop." *New York City Department of Parks and Recreation.* Retrieved 11 January 2007. www.nycgovparks.org/sub_things_to_do/events/output_pages/all_events.php?id = 32130.

"Kingsland Homestead." *Queens Historical Society.* Retrieved 11 January 2007. www.queenshistoricalsociety.org/kingsland.html.

"Kingsland Homestead, Weeping Beech Park." *New York City Department of Parks and Recreation.* Retrieved 25 March 2007.

"Houdini Bust." *Houdini.org.* Retrieved 24 March 2007. www.houdini.org/houdinibuststory.html.

"Houdini's Death." *Houdini Tribute.* Retrieved 23 March 2007. www.houdinitribute.com/death.html.

"The Houdini Seance." *About: Paranormal Phenomena.* Retrieved 23 March 2007. paranormal.about.com/library/weekly/aa103000b.htm.

"Harry Houdini." *Morbid Curiosity: Celebrity Tombstones across America.* Retrieved 23 March 2007. www.morbid-curiosity.com/id135.htm.

"Vampire." *Creatures of the Night.* Retrieved 27 March 2007. www.unexplainedstuff.com/Mysterious-Creatures/Creatures-of-the-Night.html.

"Stephen Kaplan." *Wikipedia.* Retrieved 26 March 2007. en.wikipedia.org/wiki/Stephen_Kaplan.

Wynhausen, Elisabeth. "Vampires: A Pain in the Neck." *Advertiser.* 14 March 1987. Retrieved 26 March 2007. www.adam.com.au/bstett/SupernatVampiresPain31.htm.

Stirling, Loyal. "Stephen Kaplan." *Players: For the Progressive Gamer.* Retrieved 26 March 2007. www.fortunecity.com/rivendell/final/232/kaplan.htm.

"Yes Virginia, There Are Vampires!" *Skeptic Files.* Retrieved 26 March 2007. www.skepticfiles.org/mys5/vampire1.htm.

"Staten Island." *Wikipedia.* Retrieved 29 April 2007. en.wikipedia.org/wiki/Staten_Island.

"Historic Richmond Town—Village Map." *Historic Richmond Town.* Retrieved 17 April 2007. www.historicrichmondtown.org/village_map.html.

"Historic Richmond Town—Welcome." *Historic Richmond Town.* Retrieved 17 April 2007. www.historicrichmondtown.org/index.html.

Farinacci, Amanda. "Staten Island Kicks Off First Annual Film Festival." *NY1 News.* Retrieved 17 April 2007. www.ny1.com/ny1/content/index.jsp?stid = 11&aid = 59854.

ThousandHats (blog). "Scared! Episode 10: The Parsonage." Retrieved 17 April 2007. audience.withoutabox.com/films/Scared.

Schatzman, Wendy B. "A Stroll through Richmond Town." *TravelMole Special Features News.* 3 November 2006. Retrieved 17 April 2007. www.travelmole.com/stories/1113801.php?mpnlog = 1.

Shady. "Staten Island Monastery." Lost Destinations. Retrieved 9 February 2007. www.lostdestinations.com/mnastry2.htm.

"Staten Island Monastery." *Abandoned but Not Forgotten.* Retrieved 4 April 2007. www.abandonedbutnotforgotten.com/staten_island_monastery.htm.

Walsh, Kevin. "Austen Powers: Clear Comfort, Staten Island." *Forgotten NY.* Retrieved 10 April 2007. www.forgotten-ny.com/STREET%20SCENES/austen/austen.html.

Bibliography

"Alice Austen: Her Life and Times." *Alice Austen: Her Life and Times.* Retrieved 10 April 2007. www.aliceausten.8m.com/alice/bio3.html.

"Clear Comfort: A History of the House." Retrieved 10 April 2007. www.aliceausten.8m.com/house/history.html.

"Alice Austen House." *Historic Landmark: Are We There Yet?* Retrieved 10 April 2007. www.aliceausten.org/museum.

"Alice Austen House." *Google Earth Community.* Retrieved 12 March 2007. bbs.keyhole.com/ubb/showthreaded.php/Number/684439.

"Clear Comfort." *Alice Austen House: A National Historic Landmark.* Retrieved 12 March 2007. aliceausten.org/house/index.html.

"Moravian Cemetery, Staten Island." *Wikipedia.* Retrieved 9 April 2007. en.wikipedia.org/wiki/Moravian_Cemetery.

"Tennessee Claflin." *Picture History.* Retrieved 9 April 2007. www.picturehistory.com/find/p/21214/mcm.html.

"Cornelius Vanderbilt." *Wikipedia.* Retrieved 9 April 2007. en.wikipedia.org/wiki/Cornelius_Vanderbilt.

Percy, Jr. Preston. "The Vanderbilt Mausoleum on Staten Island, New York City." *Magazine Antiques.* 1 September 2005. Retrieved 4 April 2007. www.encyclopedia.com/printable.aspx?id = 1G1:137144780.

"Tennessee Claflin." *Wikipedia.* Retrieved 18 April 2007. en.wikipedia.org/wiki/Tennessee_Claflin.

"12.Moravian Cemetery." *Staten Island History Tour Route.* Retrieved 9 April 2007. www.nypl.org/branch/staten/history/siphototour.html#12.

Walsh, Kevin. "The Dead Hill." *Forgotten NY.* Retrieved 9 April 2007. www.forgotten-ny.com/YOU'D%20NEVER%20BELIEVE/todthill/todthill.html.

Prodigal Borough, CvB, amyzeats, Kevin, Maureen Seaberg. "The Mob and the Mansion: A Brutal Murder in Kreischerville." *Prodigal Borough.* 13 May 2006. Retrieved 12 February 2007. prodigalborough.com/blogger/2006/05/mob-and-mansion-brutal-murder-in.htm.

"20m Tag on Staten Island Properties Listed by M&M." *Real Estate Weekly.* Retrieved 14 February 2007. calbears.findarticles.com/p/articles/mi_m3601/is_40_51/ai_n13790889/print.

eddygregory. "Kreischer House Site/Senior Housing." *New York Built Environment.* 30 April 2001. Retrieved 14 February 2007. groups.yahoo.com/group/newyorkbuiltenvironment/message/423.

Murda4Hire. "Kreischer Mansion." *GhostStudy.com.* 27 July 2005. Retrieved 12 February 2007. www.paranormalsoup.com/forums/lofiversion/index.php?t10855.html.

"More Haunted Crime Scenes Adding a Ghost." *Court TV Crime Library.* Retrieved 12 February 2007. www.crimelibrary.com/notorious_murders/classics/haunted_crime_scene2/2.html.

"Bigfoot in New York?" Retrieved 23 March 2007. www.angelfire.com/ny4/nyout/nybf.html.

Modem, Tom. "Trashquatch: The Hunt for Staten Island's Bigfoot."
New York Press. Retrieved 23 March 2007.
www.nypress.com/16/18/news&columns/feature.cfm.

Perry, John. "Sasquatch in New England." *BFRO: The Bigfoot Field
Researchers Organization.* Retrieved 23 March 2007.
www.bfro.net/NEWS/newengland.asp.

"Garibaldi-Meucci Museum." Home. Retrieved 31 March 2007.
www.garibaldimeuccimuseum.org/index.html.

"Ghost Hunter's University at the Garibaldi-Meucci Museum."
Ghost Hunter's University. Retrieved 31 March 2007.
www.garibaldimeuccimuseum.org/ghosthuntersuniv.html.

Perreault, John. "Ghosts of Staten Island." *Artopia.*
www.artsjournal.com/artopia/2005/09/ghosts_of_staten_island.html.

"Sailors' Snug Harbor: A World within a Fence." *Sailors' Snug Harbor.*
Retrieved 23 March 2007. www.snug-harbor.org/#fence.

"Snug Harbor Cultural Center: A Future for the Past." *Creation of Snug
Harbor Cultural Center.* Retrieved 23 March 2007.
www.snug-harbor.org/#future.

"Welcome to The Conference House." *The Conference House.*
Retrieved 3 April 2007. www.theconferencehouse.org/index.html.

"Tottenville, Staten Island." *Answers.com.* Retrieved 27 April 2007.
www.answers.com/topic/tottenville-staten-island.

"Billup House, Staten Island." The Cold Spot: Documentaries. Retrieved
31 March 2007. www.theflagship.net/coldspot/docs/
hauntedhistory-newyork.html.

"Billop House (aka Conference House)." *Long Island Paranormal
Investigators.* Retrieved 3 April 2007.
www.liparanormalinvestigators.com/nyc.shtml.

Stroming, Jason. "Conference House Field Trip 9/10/06."
Eastern Paranormal Investigations Center. Retrieved 3 April 2007.
www.epicparanormal.com/ch_9_10_06.htm.

"Conference House." *Wikipedia.* Retrieved 24 April 2006.
en.wikipedia.org/wiki/Conference_House.

"Port Richmond, Staten Island." *Wikipedia.* Retrieved 28 April 2007.
en.wikipedia.org/wiki/Port_Richmond,_Staten_Island.

Atticus. "Ghosts 2 Ghosts: Killer Ghosts." *UK Ghost Hunters.*
Retrieved 10 April 2007. www.ghost2ghosts.co.uk/
ghost-story-article.php?ghoststory = 5.

"Bayonne Bridge." *Answers.com.* Retrieved 28 April 2007.
www.answers.com/topic/bayonne-bridge-2.

Acknowledgments

I THANK MY EDITOR, KYLE WEAVER, FOR HIS FRIENDLY GUIDANCE AND expertise, editorial assistant Brett Keener for having my back, and all the others at Stackpole Books for providing me with continuing opportunities to be part of the *Haunted* state series. Yet again, I thank artist Heather Adel Wiggins, whose supernatural images grace the cover and pages of this book. But mostly, of course, I thank my wonderful family for their continuing patience and encouragement of this unusual pastime of mine: my husband, Leland Farnsworth II; my daughters, Michelle, Jamie, Katie, and Nicole; my parents, Tom and Jean Dishaw; and my siblings, Tom Dishaw, Christina Walker, and Cindy "CJ" Barry. I love you all.

About the Author

CHERI REVAI IS THE AUTHOR OF THE BEST-SELLING, THREE-BOOK SERIES *Haunted Northern New York*, as well as *Haunted Connecticut*, *Haunted Massachusetts*, and *Haunted New York*. She is a North Country native and has traveled extensively to every nook and cranny of her beloved home state of New York and its surrounds. Revai lives in northern New York with her family and a menagerie of pets. She is a mother of four, a secretary, and an author with a passion for research and history. Her website at www.theghostauthor.com provides more information on her books and upcoming projects.